THE GREAT BIG BOOK OF SHAKESPEARE QUOTES

Your Guide to Shakespeare's Greatest Quotables and Quips

William Shakespeare

To lovers of Shakespeare, quotes and all.

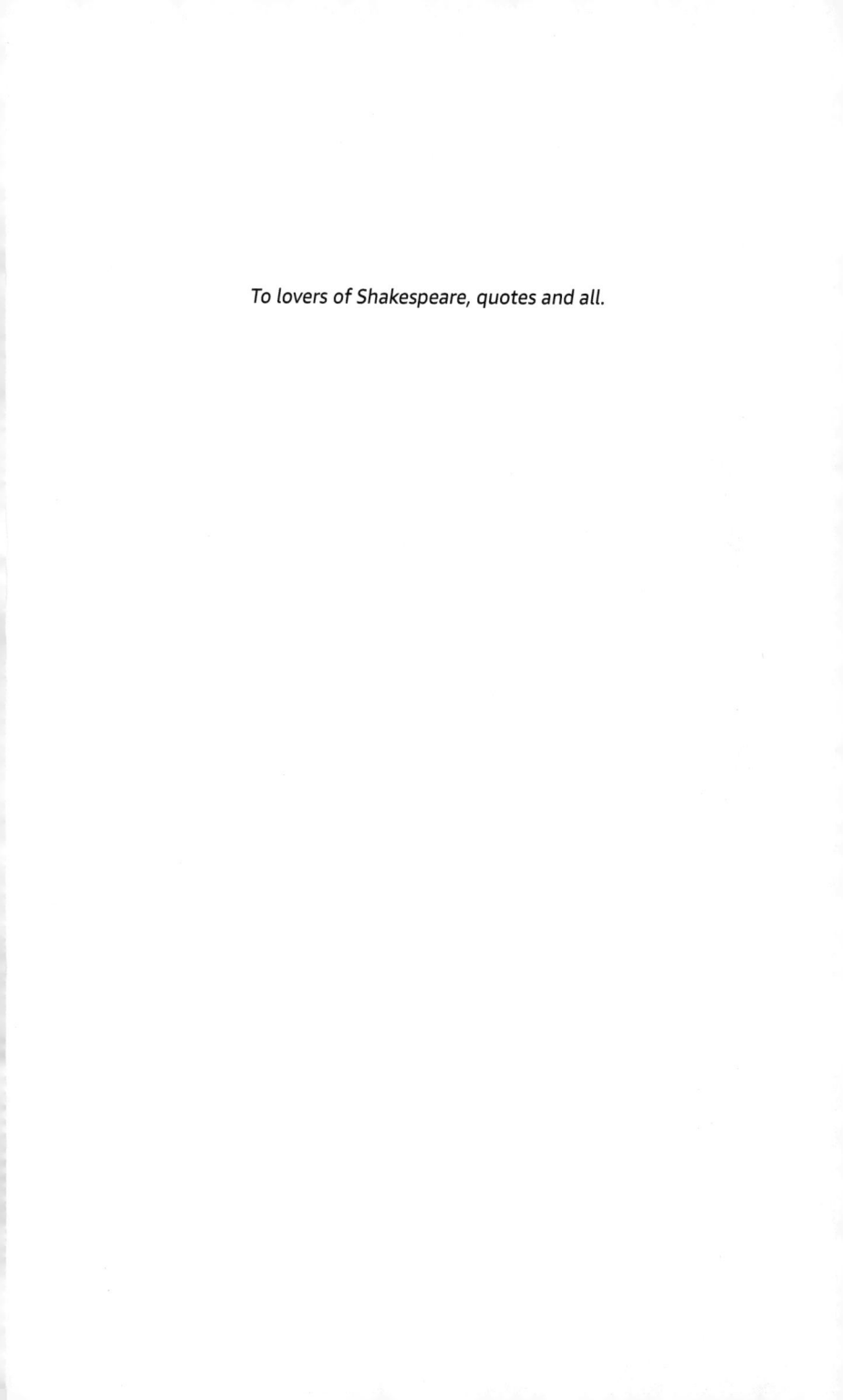

CONTENTS

Title Page

Dedication

Introduction: Measuring Greatness

Shakespeare's 20 Greatest Quotes for Almost any Occasion	1
Comedies	3
A Midsummer Night's Dream	5
Much Ado about Nothing	8
The Comedy of Errors	11
The Two Gentlemen Of Verona	14
The Merry Wives of Windsor	18
The Taming of the Shrew	21
All's Well That Ends Well	26
Twelfth Night	29
As you Like It	32
Loves Labour Lost	38
The Winter's Tale	40

Pericles, Prince of Tyre	47
The Tempest	52
The Merchant of Venice	54
Measure for Measure	59
The Tragedies	63
Antony and Cleopatra	65
Coriolanus	73
Hamlet, Prince of Denmark	80
King Lear	93
Macbeth	99
Othello	105
Julius Caesar	111
Romeo and Juliet	117
Timon of Athens	124
Cymbeline	129
Troilus and Cressida	134
Titus Andronicus	141
The Histories	145
King John	147
Richard II	152
Henry IV Part 1	158
Henry the IV Part 2	164
Henry the V	170
Henry VI Part 1	175

Henry VI Part 2	179
Henry VI Part 3	185
Richard III	192
Henry the VIII	197
Soliloquies	203
Sonnets	214
Venus and Adonis	220
The Rape of Lucrece	226
Quotes by Category	228
Ambition	230
Arrogance	231
Attitude	232
Beauty	233
Business	234
Bravery, Courage and Caution	235
Curses and Insults	236
Education and Learning	238
Ethics and Villainy	239
Friends and Friendship	240
Giving	242
Fame and Fate	243
Grieving and Sorrow	244
Honesty	246
Honor and integrity	247

Home	248
Hope	249
Indiscretion	250
Judgment and Justice	251
Killing and death	252
Language, Words, and Communication	254
Love and Lust	256
Men and Women	262
Money	266
News	267
Opinion	268
Passion	269
Peace	270
Pleasure	271
Revenge	272
Reason	273
Truth	274
Understanding	276
War	278
Wisdom	280
Youth	282
Books By This Author	283

INTRODUCTION: MEASURING GREATNESS

Not all of Wayne Gretzky's greatest goals came in championship games and not all of Caesar's victories were monumental. There were great goals in many not-so great games and many brilliant decisions in minor victories. Both Gretzky and Caesar are still considered the greatest of their craft. To ignore the great moments they had in not-so-great confrontations would be ignorant and unjust.

Indeed, without the great moments in minor deeds, no icon of culture would have attain greatness. Like a Monet Painting, the brilliant dots of achievement throughout a life or body of work create the final grand tapestry of greatness.

Greatness is never just a single victory or a single moment of brilliance. The same is more true for Shakespeare; his greatness can be found in all his works. When we gloss over his great lines in his lesser known art, we miss a very vital part of what his true greatness entails. True greatness is performing beyond the average in all ventures. Therefore, it is natural that all of Shakespeare's works have some great lines in them. Even his modestly appreciated works would overshadow any competitor in playwriting today and his supreme works that we all know- Romeo and Juliet, Hamlet, King Lear- also obscure his less popular works. It's a beautiful tragedy. What is the loss?

Imagine never looking at the stars because the sun is just dominantly bright and beautiful; we'd miss a lot of heavenly glory that creation has gifted us. That would be a tragedy of Shakespearean proportions. And that's what the world does to

Shakespeare. We know his greatest lines from his greatest works, but gloss over the others because of ignorance or a lack of appreciation or simply from not enough time to recognize them. What an incredible loss for us all.

To help illuminate more of his greatness, here are Shakespeare's greatest lines- at least my take as a literature lover, teacher, and a student of philosophy- including the brilliant stars dwarfed by his greatest works. Brilliant, beautiful lines from Troilus and Cressida, Henry the IV Part 1, Measure for Measure, The Rape of Lucrece, and all the others. Seize them and enjoy them- they're uncommon treasure lying right under our noses. By getting to know them, we obtain a real wealth the casual fan of Shakespeare will never know.

I hope you love these quotes (and Henry the IV Part 1, my favorite play) as much as I do. If just one person starts to enjoy Shakespeare just a little more because of this book, I'll consider a goal attained.

To enjoy Shakespeare via this book, I have organized it by type of work (play, sonnet, narrative poem) and organized the plays into category of play type. The end of the book is quotes organized by subject matter, with a conscious effort to avoid cross-categorizing quotes, even though many fit well into different categories. You can search for quotes by the play title or by the subject matter of the quote using the impressively (excessively?) long table of contents.

One other note about format: In general, I've kept the quotes as true to the original format as possible. If a quote begins part way through a line or was from a section of blank verse (10 syllables per line), I've generally kept it that way for truer reading, though not always as a means of conserving space (and printing costs). I've also added capitals and periods in some spaces to make the format easier on our modern eyes.

The idea of any work commenting on Shakespeare is to increase understanding and enjoyment, and not necessarily in that order. Pick an interesting section, dive in, and enjoy.

Thank you.

Ben Nelson

SHAKESPEARE'S 20 GREATEST QUOTES FOR ALMOST ANY OCCASION

1. We know what we are but not what we may be. – Hamlet
2. Love is not love which alters when it alteration finds.- Sonnet 116
3. The course of true love never did run smooth.- A Midsummer Night's Dream
4. Wisdom cries out in the street and no man regards it- Henry the IV part 1
5. To thine own self be true.- Hamlet
6. Nothing will come of nothing. – King Lear
7. There is no art to find the mind's construction in the face. – Macbeth
8. Some rise by sin, and some by virtue fall. - Measure for Measure
9. Love is merely a madness- As You Like it.
10. The fool doth think he is wise, but the wise man knows himself to be a fool. – As You Like It
11. I confess nothing, I deny nothing.- Much Ado about Nothing.
12. Love sought is good but given unsought is better. -Twelfth Night.
13. Young blood doth not obey an old decree. - Love's Labour's Lost.

14. Mirth cannot move a soul in agony.- Love's Labour's Lost.
15. He that dies pays all debts!- The Tempest.
16. Nature's above art- King Lear.
17. Sad hours seem long. – Romeo and Juliet.
18. To see how God in all his creatures works!- Henry VI part 2.
19. Is not the truth the truth? - Henry IV part 1.
20. I cannot hide what I am.- Much Ado About Nothing.

COMEDIES

Modern comedy films and plays have a largely different meaning from the title when used to refer to Shakespeare's plays. A comedy, when referring to Shakespeare, is a story with a happy ending for the protagonist. If it is not tragic, and not historical, it qualifies as happy and therefore a comedy. While there are some plays that we wouldn't consider, "happy endings" (Measure for Measure, Pericles) perhaps we are just too spoiled by modern cinema and modern life.

In the 1600's, if life continued, perhaps that was enough to adopt a disposition of happiness as your automatic perspective of life. As Shakespeare's gravedigger states in Hamlet, "What should a man do but be merry?"

That is a great default position. If a play ends with the protagonist still having a chance at future happiness, it is a comedy. Enjoy!

Order of the comedies:

Midsummer Night's Dream
Much Ado about Nothing
Comedy of Errors
Two Gentlemen of Verona
The Merry Wives of Windsor

Taming of the Shrew
All's well that End's Well
Twelfth Night
As You Like it
Comedy of Errors
Love's Labour Lost
The Winter's Tale
Pericles, Prince of Tyre
The Tempest
The Merchant of Venice
Measure for Measure

A MIDSUMMER NIGHT'S DREAM

You have her father's love, Demetrius;
let me have Hermia's; do you marry him.
1.1.93-94.

The course of true love never did run smooth.
1.1.127.

Sickness is catching; O, were favour so
Yours would I catch, fair Hermia, ere I go.
1.1.186-187.

I give him curses, yet he gives me love.
1.1.196.

As waggish boys in game themselves forswear,
So the boy love is perjur'd everywhere.
1.1.240-241.

You may do it extempore, for it is nothing but roaring.
1.2.60.

I will aggravate my voice so, that I will roar you as gently as any suckling dove.
1.2.73-74.

These are the forgeries of jealousy.
2.1.81.

Do you amend it then; it lies in you.
2.1.118.

The juice of it on sleeping eyelids laid
Will make or man or woman madly dote
Upon the next live creature that it sees.

2.1.170-172.

I am sick when I look not on you.
2.1.214.

You draw me, you hard-hearted adamant;
But yet you draw not iron, for my heart
is true as steel. Leave you your power to draw,
and I shall have no power to follow you.
2.1.194-198.

We cannot fight for love as men may do;
We should be woo'd and were not make to woo.
2.1.241-242.

On heart, one bed, two bosoms, on troth.
2.2.42.

My heart unto yours I knit.
2.2.48.

No; I do repent
The tedious minutes I have with her spent.
2.2.111-112.

Tempt not too much the hatred of my spirit;
for I am sick when I do look on you.
2.2.212-213

Oh, why rebuke him that loves you so?
3.1.43.

And yet, to say the truth, reason and love keep little company together now-a-days.
3.1.133-134

Though she be but little, she is fierce.
3.1.325.

This their jangling I esteem sport.
3.1.353.

My mistress with a monster is in love.

3.2.6.

Scorn and derision never come in tears.
3.2.123.

Look when I vow, I weep; and vows so born,
in their nativity all truth appears.
3.2.124-125.

I would I had your bond; for I perceive
a weak bond holds you, I'll not trust your word
3.2.266-267.

Be as thou wast wont to be;
see as thou was wont to see.
4.1.68-69.

Are you sure that we are awake? It seems to me that yet we sleep,
we dream.
4.1.190-191.

I have had a most rare vision.
4.1.198.

I have had a dream, past the wit of man to say what dream it was.
Man is but an ass if he go about to expound this dream.
4.1.198-200.

How shall we find the concord of this discord?
5.1.60.

This is the greatest error of all the rest.
5.1.239.

With the help of a surgeon he might yet recover and yet prove an
ass.
5.1.200.

MUCH ADO ABOUT NOTHING

In our last conflict four of his five wits went halting off, and now the whole man is govr'ned with one.
1.1.53-4.

Courtesy itself must convert to disdain if you come in her presence.
1.1.102-103.

I had rather hear my dog bark at a crow than rather hear a man swear that he loves me.
1.1.111-112.

I cannot hide what I am.
1.3.10

He that hath no beard is less than a man
2.1.29.

Grow this to what adverse issue it can, I will put it in practice.
2.3.47.

I do much wonder that one man, seeing how much another man is a fool when he dedicates his behaviours to love, will, after he hath laugh'd at such shallow follies in others, become the argument of his won scorn by falling in love.
2.3.7-10.

Happy are they that hear their detractions and put them to mending.
2.3.207-208.

A man loves the meat in his youth that he cannot endure in his age.
2.3.218-219.

When I said I would die a bachelor, I did not think I should lie till

I were married.
2.3.221-222.

Some cupid kills with arrows, some with traps.
3.1.106.

To be a well-favoured man is the gift of fortune; but to write and read comes by nature.
3.3.13-14.

When rich villains have need of poor ones, poor ones may make what price they will.
3.3.104-105.

Comparisons are odorous.
3.5.15.

O, what men dare do! What men may do! What men daily do, not knowing what they do!
4.1.144-155.

For my part, I am so attir'd in wonder, I know not what to say.
4.1.144-145.

That what we have we prize not the worth Whiles we enjoy it, but being lack'd and lost, Why, then we rack the value, then we find the virtue that possession would not show us whiles it was our.
4.1.218-222.

I do love nothing in the world so well as you. Is not that strange?
4.1.266-267.

I confess nothing, I deny nothing.
4.1.270.

You dare easier be friends with me than fight with mine enemy.
4.1.296.

Men can counsel and speak comfort to that grief which they themselves not feel; but, tasting it, their counsel turns to passion, which before would give precipitable medicine to rage.
5.1.20-24.

Tis all men's office to speak patience to those who wring under the load of sorrow, but no man's virtue nor sufficiency to be so moral when he shall endure the like himself.
5.1.27-31.

There was never yet philosopher that could endure the toothache.
5.1.35-36.

In a false quarrel there is no valour.
5.1.119.

If a man do not erect him this age his own tomb ere he dies, eh shall live no longer in monument than the bell rings and the widow weeps.
5.2.67-68.

Here's our own hands against our heart.
5.4.91.

A college of wit crackers cannot flout me out of my humor.
5.4.99-100.

THE COMEDY OF ERRORS

Yet this my comfort; when your words are done,
My woes end likewise with the evening sun.
1.1.26-27.

He that commends me to mine own content
Commends me to the thing I cannot get.
1.2.33-34.

Nay, he struck so plainly I could too well feel his blows; and withal so doubtfully that I could scarce understand them.
2.1.51-52.

Self-harming jealousy!
2.1.102.

How many mad fools serve mad jealousy.
2.1.116.

What error drives our eyes and ears amiss?
2.1.182.

There's no time for a man to recover his hair that grows bald by nature.
2.2.71.

Until I know this sure uncertainty,
I'll entertain the offer'd fallacy.
2.2.184-185.

If the skin were parchment, and the blows you gave were ink, your own handwriting would tell you what I think.
3.1.12-13.

Herein you war against your reputation.
3.1.86.

For slander lives upon succession
For ever hous'd where it gets possession.
3.1.105-106.

Shall love, in building, grow so ruinous?
3.2.6.

What simple thief brags of his own attaint?
3.2.16.

Ill deed is doubled with an evil word.
3.2.20.

What claim lays she to thee?
Marry, sir, such claim as you would lay to your horse; and she would have me as a beast; not that, I being a beast, she would have me; but that she, being a very beastly creature, lays claim to me.
3.2.83-87.

I have but lean luck in the match and yet is she a wondrous fat marriage.
3.2.91-92.

Marry sir, she's the kitchen-wench, and all grease; and I know not what use to put her to but to make a lamp of her and run from her by her own light. I warrant, her rags and the tallow in them will burn a Poland winter. If she lives till doomsday, she'll burn a week longer than the whole world.
3.2.93-99.

No longer from head to foot than from hip to hip; she is spherical, like a globe; I could fin dout countries in her.
3.2.113-114.

As from a bear a man would run for his life,
So fly I from her that would be my wife.
3.2.152-153.

No evil lost is eve wai'd when it is gone.
4.2.24.

Time is a very bankrupt and owes more than he's worth to season.
4.2.58.

There's not a man I meet but doth salute me
As if I were there well-acquainted friend.
4.3.1-2.

Some blessed power deliver us from hence.
4.3.38.

Thou whoreson, senseless villain.
4.3.23.

I know it by their pale and deadly looks.
4.4.90.

The venom clamours of a jealous woman
Poisons more deadly than a mad dog's tooth.
5.1.69-70.

Unquiet meals make ill digestions.
5.1.74.

THE TWO GENTLEMEN OF VERONA

Home keeping youths have ever homely wits.
1.1.2.

Yet writers say, as in the sweetest bud the eating canker dwells, so eating love inhabits the finest wits of all.
1.1.42-43.

I leave myself, my friends, and all for love.
1.1.65.

They do not love that do not show their love.
1.2.31.

O, they love least that let men know their love.
1.2.32.

Experience is by industry achieved,
and perfected by the swift course of time.
1.3.23-24.

Thus have I shunn'd the fire for fear of burning,
and drench'd me in the sea, where I am drown'd.
1.3.78-79.

Love is blind.
2.1.63.

Parting strikes poor lovers dumb.
2.2.21.

Love's a mighty lord,
and hath so humbled me as I confess
there is no woe to his correction

nor to his service no such joy on earth.
2.4.132-135.

When I was sick you gave me bitter pills,
and I must minister the like to you.
2.4.145-146.

For love, thou knowest, is full of jealousy.
2.4.173.

Unheedful vows may heedfully be broken
2.6.11.

Thou wouldst as soon go kindle fire with snow
as seek to quench the fire of love with words.
2.7.19-20.

My duty pricks me on to utter that
which else no worldly good should draw from me.
3.1.9-10.

Dumb jewels often in their silent kind
more than quick words do move a woman's mind.
3.1.91-92.

A woman sometime scorns what best contents her.
3.1.93.

That man that hath a tongue, I say, is no man
if with his tongue he cannot win a woman.
3.1.104-105.

To be slow in words is a woman's only virtue.
3.1.33-336.

Hope is a lover's staff.
3.1.245.

I am but a fool.
3.1.261.

Cease to lament for that thou canst not help,
and study help for that which thou lament'st.
3.1.241-242.

She hath more hair than wit, and more faults than hairs, and more wealth than faults.
3.1.344-345.

Where your good word cannot advantage him,
your slander never can endamage him;
3.2.42-43.

Much is the force of heaven-bred poesy.
3.2.72.

The more she spurns my love
The more it grows and fawneth on her still.
4.2.14-15.

Love will creep in service where it cannot go.
4.2.19-20.

How now, you whoreson peasant?
4.4.39-40.

Think'st thou I am so shallow, so conceitless,
to be seduced by thy flattery,
that hast deceiv'd so many with thy vows?
4.2.92-95.

Alas, how love can trifle with itself!
4.4.179.

Love will not be spurred to what it loathes.
5.1.7.

How use doth breed a habit in a man!
5.4.1.

By my coming I have made you happy
5.4.30.

By thy approach thou mak'st me most unhappy.
5.4.31.

In love, who respects friend?
5.4.54.

The private wound is deepest.
5.4.71.

It is the lesser blot, modesty finds,
Women to change their shapes than men their minds.
5.4.108-109.

O heaven, were man but constant, he were perfect!
5.4.111.

Twere pity two such friends should be long foes.
5.4.118.

I hold him but a fool that will endanger his body
For a girl that loves him not.
5.4.133-134.

THE MERRY WIVES OF WINDSOR

It is not meet the council hear a riot; there is no fear of God in a riot.
1.1.32.

He hath studied her well, and translated her will out of honesty into English.
1.3.46.

Let vultures gripe thy guts!
1.3.82.

We burn daylight.
2.1.34.

I think the best way were to entertain him with hope till the wicked fire of lust have melted him in his own grease.
2.1.57-58.

There's the short and the long.
2.1.118.

Why, then the worlds my oyster. Which I with sword will open.
2.2.4-5.

Old folks, you know, have discretion as they say, and know the world.
2.2.117-118.

Love like a shadow flies when shadow love pursues;
pursuing that that flies, and flying what pursues.
2.2.187-188.

See the hell of of having a false woman
2.2.256.

The rankest compound of villainous smell that ever offended nostril.
2.5.83.

Disarm them; let them keep their limbs whole and hack our English.
3.1.70-71.

Thou must be thyself
3.4.3.

Alas, I had rather be set quick I' the earth and bowl'd to death with turnips.
3.4.85-86.

You do ill to teach the child such words.
4.1.60.

The devil take one party and his dam the other.
4.5.98.

I hope good luck lies in odd numbers.
5.1.2.

O powerful love, that in some respects makes a beast a man and in some other a man a beast.
5.5.3-4.

When gods have hot backs what shall poor men do?
5.5.10.

I think the devil will not have me damn'd, lest the oil that's in me should set hell on fire; he would never else cross me thus.
5.5.32-33.

Fairies use flowers for their charactery.
5.5.71.

See now how wit may be made a jack-a-lent when 'tis upon ill employment.
5.5.123.

In love, the heavens themselves do guide the sates;

money buys lands, and wives are sold by fate.
5.5.219-220.

THE TAMING OF THE SHREW

And if the boy have not a woman's gift to rain a shower of commanded tears, an onion will do well for such a shift.
Introduction: 1.1.122-224.

Affection is not rated from the heart;
If love have touch'd you, nought remains but so.
1.1.155-156.

If it be so, sir, that you are the man
Must stead us all, and me amongst the rest;
And if you break the ice, and do this feat
Achieve the elder and set the younger free
For our access—whose hap shall be to have her
Will not so graceless be to be ingrate.
1.2.261-265.

O, that a mighty man of such decent,
of such possessions, and so high esteem,
should be infused with so foul a spirit!
Introduction:1.2.13-15.

Thou art a lord, and nothing but a lord.
Introduction:1.2.59.

No profit grows where is no pleasure ta'en;
in brief sir, study wat you most affect.
1.1.39-40.

I pray, sir, tell me, is it possible
that love should of a sudden take such hold?
1.1.142-142.

Sufficeth, my reasons are both good and weighty.
1.1.241.

Such wind as scatters young men through the world to seek their fortunes farther than at home where small experience grows.
1.2.48-50.

'Twixt such friends as we few words suffice.
1.2.63-64.

Why nothing comes amiss, so money come withal.
1.2.79-80.

I would not wed her for a mine of gold.
1.2.90.

He hath the jewel of my life in hold.
1.2.117.

Mistake me not; I speak but as I find.
2.1.66.

I doubt it not sir, but you will curse your wooing.
2.1.75.

And where two raging fires meet together,
they do consume the thing that feeds their fury.
2.1.130-131.

Though little fire grows great with little wind,
Yet extreme gust will blow out ire and all.
2.1.133-134.

Be thou arm'd for some unhappy words.
2.1.138.

Asses are made to bear and so are you.
2.1.198.

Women are made to bear, and so are you.
2.1.199.

And will you, nill you, I will marry you.
2.1.263.

And may not young men die as well as old?
2.1.383.

Preposterous ass, that never read so far, to know the cause why music was ordain'd was it not to refresh the mind of man after his studies or his usual pain?
3.1.8-11.

I'll not be tied to hours nor pointed times,
But learn my lessons as I please myself.
3.1.19-20.

Old fashions please me best; I am not so nice
to change true rules for odd inventions.
3.1.78-79.

To me she's married, not unto my clothes.
3.1.113.

I will be master of what is mine own.
3.1.225.

I must, forsooth, be forc'd to give my hand, oppos'd against my heart, unto a mad-brain rudesby.
3.2.8-10.

He's a devil, a devil, a very fiend.

Why, she's a devil, a devil, the devil's dam.
3.2.151-152.

Winter tames man, woman, and beast.
4.1.21.

You whoreson villain.
4.1.139.

You heedless joltheads and unmanner'd slaves!
4.1.150.

Go, get thee gone, thou false, deluding slave.
4.1.31.

Kindness in women, not their beauteous looks, shall win my love.
4.2.40-41.

My tongue will tell the anger of my heart,
or else my heart concealing it, will beak.
4.3.77-78.

And as the sun breaks through the darkest clouds,
so honor peereth in the meanest habit.
4.3.169-170.

Happy the parents of so fair a child.
4.5.38.

Sir, you seem a sober, ancient gentleman by your habit, but your words show you a madman.
5.1.62-63.

Better once than never, for never too late.
5.1.135.

'He that is giddy thinks the world turns around'
5.2.26.

The fouler fortune mine, and there's an end.
5.2.98.

A woman mov'd is like a fountain troubled.
5.2.142.

Too little payment for so great a debt.
5.2.153.

I am asham'd that women are so simple to offer war where they should kneel for peace.
5.2.161-162.

ALL'S WELL THAT ENDS WELL

Moderate lamentation is the right of the dead: excessive grief the enemy to the living.
1.1.48.

Love all, trust a few, do wrong to none.
1.1.57-58.

Full often we see cold wisdom waiting on superfluous folly.
1.1.99-100.

Man is enemy to virginity; how may we barricade it against him?
1.1.106.

It is not politic in the commonwealth of nature to preserve virginity.
1.1.118-119.

'Tis a commodity will lose the gloss with lying; the longer kept, the less worth.
1.1.141-143.

Get thee a good husband and use him as he uses thee.
1.1.199.

Since I nor wax nor honey can bring home,
I quickly were dissolved from my hive
To give some labourers rooms.
1.2.64-66.

Our remedies oft in ourselves do lie,
which we ascribe to heaven.
1.1.202-203.

We wound our modesty, and make foul the clearness of our

deservings, when of ourselves we publish them.
1.3.6-7.

I am driven on by the flesh; and he must needs go that the devil drives.
1.3.27-28.

That man should be at woman's command, and yet no hurt done!
1.3.87.

It is the show and seal of nature's truth,
where love's strong passion is impress'd in youth.
1.3.123-124.

Invention is asham'd against the proclamation of thy passion.
1.3.164-165.

Only sin and hellish obstinacy tie thy tongue, that truth should be suspected.
1.3.170-172.

My friends were poor, but honest; so's my love.
1.3.186.

Oft expectations fails, and most oft there
where most it promises; and oft it hits
where hope is coldest, and despair fits most.
2.1.141-143.

A young man married is a young man that's marr'd
2.3.291.

She is too mean to have her name repeated.
3.5.57.

What things we are!
4.3.18.

How mightily sometimes we make us comforts of our losses!
4.3.61.

Our virtues would be merry if our faults whipt them not; and our crimes would despair if they were not cherish'd by our virtues.
4.3.70-72.

He has everything that an honest man should not have
4.3.241-242.

Praising what is lost makes the remembrance dear.
5.3.19-20.

To the brightest beams distracted clouds give way.
5.1.33-34.

Our rash faults make trivial price of serious things we have.
5.3.60.

Oft our pleasures, to ourselves unjust,
destroy our friends, and after weep their dust.
5.3.63-64.

This woman's an easy love, my lord; she goes off and on pleasure.
5.3.271.

And if it end so meet,
the bitter past, more welcome is the sweet.
5.3.325-326.

TWELFTH NIGHT

If music be the food of love, play on.
1.1.1.

Away before me to sweet beds of flow'rs;
Love-thoughts lie rich when canopied with bow'rs.
1.1.40.

When my tongue blabs, then let mine eyes not see.
1.2.63.

These clothes are good enough to drink in, and so be these boots too.
1.3.9-10.

He that is well hang'd in this world needs to fear no colours.
1.5.3.

Better a witty fool than a foolish wit.
1.5.33.

Infirmity, that decays the wise, doth ever make the better fool.
1.5.71-72.

Sure, you have some hideous matter to deliver, when the courtesy of it is so fearful.
1.5.194-195.

I shall crave of you your leave that I may bear my evils alone.
2.1.6.

Alas, our frailty is the cause, not we!
For such as we are made of, such we be.
2.1.29-30.

If you will not murder me for my love, let me be your servant.
2.1.31.

We men may say more, swear more, but indeed
our shows are more than will; for still we prove
much in our vows, but little in our love.
2.4.114-116.

Why, thou hast put him in such a dream that when the image of it leaves him he must run mad.
2.4.173-174.

Some are born great, some achieve greatness, and some have greatness thrust upon em.
2.5.129-130.

Not worthy to touch fortune's fingers.
2.5.139.

They that dally nicely with words may quickly make them wanton.
3.1.13.

I can no other answer make but thanks,
And thanks, and ever thanks.
3.3.14-15.

This fellow is wise enough to play the fool;
And to do that well craves a kind of wit.
3.1.66-67.

Tis a vulgar proof
that very oft we pity our enemies.
3.1.120-121.

Love sought is good but given unsought is better.
3.1.152.

I am mad as he,
if sad and merry madness equal be.
3.4.14-15.

What man, defy the devil; consider, he's an enemy to mankind.
3.4.93.

I say there is no darkness but ignorance
4.2.38.

Yet doth this accident and flood of fortune
so far exceed all instance, all discourse,
that I am ready to distrust mine eyes
and wrangle with my reason.
4.3.11-14.

The better for my foes and the worse for my friends.
5.1.10.

We took him for a coward, but he's the very devil incarnate.
5.1.172-173.

An apple cleft in two is not more twin than these two creatures.
5.1.215-216.

So much against the mettle of your sex
So far beneath our soft and tender breeding,
And since you call'd me master for so long,
Here is my hand; you shall from this time be
Your master's mistress.
5.1.309-313.

You have done me wrong, notorious wrong.
5.1.315-316.

I'll be revenged on the whole pack of you.
5.1.364.

AS YOU LIKE IT

The spirit of my father grows strong in me.
1.1.62.

I had as lief thou dids't break his neck as his arm.
1.1.131.

There is not one so young and so villainous this day living.
1.1.136.

Love no man in good earnest, nor do no further in sport neither than with safety of a pure blush thou mayst in honour come off again.
1.2.24-26.

Though nature hath given us wit to flout at fortune, hath not fortune sent in this fool to cut off the argument?
1.2.41-43.

The more pity that fools may not speak wisely what wise men do foolishly.
1.2.78.

Thus men may grow wiser every day.
1.2.118.

Young gentlemen, your spirits are too bold for your years.
1.2.155.

Thou prun'st a rotten tree
That cannot so much as a blossom yield
In lieu of all they pains and husbandry.
2.3.63-65.

I shall do my friends no wrong; for I have none to lament me.
1.2.171.

That which here stands up is but a quintain, a mere lifeless block.
1.2.229-230.

Nay, thy words are too precious to be cast away upon curs.
1.3.5.

You are a fool.
1.3.83.

Beauty proveth thieves sooner than gold.
1.3.106.

Hath not old custom made this life more sweet
Than that of painted pomp?
2.1.2-3.

Are not these woods more free from peril than the envious court?
2.1.3-4.

Misery doth part the flux of company.
2.1.50-51.

Sweep on, you fat and greasy citizens.
2.1.55.

O, what a world is this, when what is comely
envenoms him that bears it!
3.3.14-15.

This I must do or know not what to do
2.3.34.

O good old man, how well in thee appears
The constant service of the antique world,
When service sweat for duty, not for meed!
Thou art not for the fashion of these times,
Where none will sweat but for promotion,
And having that, do choke their service up
Even with the having: it is not so with thee.
2.3.55-60.

I care not for my spirits, if my legs were not weary.
2.4.2.

For my part, I had rather bear with you than bear you.
2.4.9-10.

When I was at home, I was in a better place;
but travellers must be content.
2.4.12-13.

We that are true lovers run into strange capers;
but as all is mortal in nature, so is all nature in love mortal in folly.
2.4.50-52.

I think he be transform'd into a beast;
for I can nowhere find him like a man.
2.7.1-2.

The wise man's folly is anatomized, even by the squand'ring glances of the fool.
2.7.55-56.

Give me leave to speak my mind, and I will through and through cleanse the foul body of th' infected world,
if they will patiently receive my medicine.
2.7.58-60.

You touch'd my vein at first: the thorny point
Of bare distress hath ta'en from me the show
of smooth civility; yet am I inland bread, and know some nurture.
2.7.93-95.

Your gentleness shall force more than your force move us to gentleness.
2.7.102-103.

This wide and universal theatre
presents more woeful pageants than the scene
wherein we play.
2.7.137-139.

In respect that it is solitary, I like it very well' but in respect that it is private,

it is a very file life.
3.2.15-17.

He that wants money, means, and content is without three good friends.
3.2.22-23.

When I think, I must speak.
3.2.234.

Will you sit down with me? And we two will rail against our mistress the world, and all our misery.
3.2.260-261.

I thank god I am not a woman, to be touch'd with so many giddy offences as he hath generally tax'd their whole sex withal.
3.2.325-326.

I will not cast away my physic but on those that are sick.
3.2.332.

Love is merely a madness; and I tell you, deserves as well a dark house and a whip as madmen do and the reason why they are not so punish'd and cured is that the lunacy is so ordinary that the whippers are in love too. Yet I profess curing it by counsel.
3.2.367-372.

Doth my simple feature content you?
3.3.2-3.

Honesty coupled to beauty is to have a sauce to sugar.
3.3.27.

The sight of lovers feedeth those in love.
3.4.53.

Sell when you can; you are not for all markets.
3.4.60.

For I am falser than vows made in wine.
3.4.72.

Those that are in extremity of either are abominable fellows,

and betray themselves to every modern censure worse than drunkards.
4.1.6-7.

Can one desire too much of a good thing?
4.1.107.

Maids are May when they are maids, but the sky changes when they are wives.
4.1.130-133.

Patience herself would startle at this letter,
And play the swaggerer. Bear this, bear all.
4.3.13-14.

Kindness, ever stronger than revenge.
4.3.127.

There is too great testimony in your complexion that it was a passion of earnest.
4.3.168-169.

By my troth, we that have good wits have much to answer for.
5.1.10-11.

Wounded it is, but with the eyes of a lady.
5.1.22.

The fool doth think he is wise, but the wise man knows himself to be a fool.
5.1.28-29.

O, how bitter a thing it is to look into happiness through another man's eyes.
5.1.39-40.

I hope it is no dishonest desire to desire to be a woman of the world.
5.3.2-3.

I hope it is no dishonest desire to desire to be a woman of the world.
5.3.3-4.

I count it but lost time to hear such a foolish song.
5.3.34-35.

Here comes a very strange pair of beasts which in all tongues are call'd fools.
5.4.37.

Rich honesty dwells like a miser, sir, in a poor house; as your pearl in your foul oyster.
5.4.57-59.

To you I give myself, I am yours.
5.4.110.

We will begin these rites,
As we do trust the'll end in true delights.
5.4.191-192.

Good plays prove the better by the help of good epilogues.
Epilogue; 5-6.

LOVES LABOUR LOST

The mind shall banquet, though the body pine.
1.1.25.

Fat paunches have lean pates; and dainty bits
Make rich the ribs, but bankrupt quite the wits.
1.1.26-27.

Love is a devil. There is not evil angel but love.
1.2.162-163.

Beauty is bought by judgment of the eye,
Not utt'red by base sale of chapmen's tongues.
2.1.14-15.

A man of sovereign parts, peerless esteem'd, well fitted in arts, glorious in arms; nothing becomes him ill that we would well.
2.1.44-46.

Not a word without him but a jest.
2.1.214.

By heart you love her, because your heart cannot come by her; in heart you love her, because your heart is in love with her; and out of heart you love her, being out of heart that you cannot enjoy her.
3.1.37-41.

To sell a bargain well is as cunning as fast and loose
3.1.97.

Fair payment for foul words is more than due.
4.1.19.

If love make me forsworn, how shall I swear to love?
4.2.100.

I fear these stubborn lines lack power to move.
4.3.51.

Young blood doth not obey an old decree.
4.3.213.

Devils soonest tempt, resembling spirits of light.
4.3.253.

I never knew man to hold vile stuff so dear.
4.3.272.

For where is any author in the world
Teaches such beauty as a woman's eye?
4.3.308-309.

Learning is but an adjunct to ourself,
And where we are our learning likewise is.
4.3.310-311.

He draweth out the thread of his verbosity finer than the staple of his argument.
5.1.14.

Folly in fools bears not so strong a note
As fool'ry in the wise when wit doth dote,
Since all the power thereof it doth apply
to prove, by wit, worth in simplicity.
5.2.75-78.

They did not bless us with one happy word.
5.2.369.

A heavy heart bears not so nimble a tongue.
5.2.725.

Honest plain words best pierce the ear of grief.
5.2.741.

Mirth cannot move a soul in agony.
5.2.845.

THE WINTER'S TALE

You pay a great deal too dear for what's given freely.
1.1.17.

I very well agree with you in the hopes of him. It is a gallant child; one that indeed physics the subject, makes old hearts fresh; they that went on crutches ere he was born desire yet their life to see him a man.
1.1.34-39.

One good deed dying tongueless
slaughters a thousand waiting upon that?
1.1.92-93.

See your face for fivepence and 'tis dear.
1.1.152.

Go play, boy, play; thy mother plays, and I play too.
1.1.187-188.

Many thousand on's
Have the disease and feel it not.
1.1.206-207.

We have been deceived in thy integrity,
deceived in that which seems so.
1.1.239-240.

Were my life's liver
infected as her life, she would not live
the running of one glass.
1.1.304-305.

There is sickness which puts some of us in distemper;
but I cannot name the disease; and it is caught
of you that yet are well.

1.1.385.

You may as well forbid the sea for to obey the moon
as or by oath remove our counsel shake the fabric of his folly,
whose foundation is pil'd upon his faith and will continue the
standing of his body.
1.1.426-431.

Sure tis safer to
avoid what is grown than question how it is born.
1.1.432-433.

This action I now go on is for my better grace.
1.2.121-122

A sad tale's best for winter.
2.1.24.

There may be in the cup
a Spider steep'd, and one may drink, depart,
and yet partake no venom, for his knowledge
is not infected; but if one present
th' abhorred ingredient to his eye, make known
how he hath drunk, he cracks his gorge, his sides,
with violent hefts. I have drunk, and seen the spider.
2.1.38-45.

A bed-swerver, even as bad as those
That vulgars give bold'st titles.
2.1.92-93.

You smell this business with a sense as cold
as is a dead man's nose.
2.1.151-152.

The silence often of pure innocence
persuades when speaking fails.
2.2.41-42.

When she shall take the rein, I let her run;
but she'll not stumble.
2.3.51-52.

This child was prisoner to the womb.
2.2.59.

It is an heretic that makes the fire,
Not she which burns in't.
2.3.113-114.

I am a feather for each wind that blows.
2.3.152.

You're liars all.
2.3.144.

A thousand knees
Ten thousand years together, naked, fasting
Upon a barren mountain, and still winder in storm perpetual could not move the gods
To look that way thou wert.
3.1.207-211.

All faults I make, when I shall come to know them,
I do repent.
3.1.215-216.

Innocence shall make a false accusation blush
3.2.28-29.

If powers divine
Behod our human actions, as they do,
I doubt not then but innocence shall make
False accusation blush, and tyranny
Tremble at patience.
3.2.26-30.

To me can life be no commodity.
3.2.91.

I have too much believ'd my own suspicion.
3.2.148.

I would there were no age between ten and three and twenty,

or that youth would sleep out the rest; for there is nothing in the between but getting wenches with child, wronging the ancientry, stealing, fighting.
3.3.1-4.

'Tis a lucky day, boy, and we'll do good deeds on it.
3.3.131.

Kings are no less unhappy, their issue not being gracious, than they are in losing them when they have approved their virtues.
4.1.25-27.

O that ever I was born!
4.1.57.

There's no virtue whipt out of the court. They cherish it to make it stay there; and yet it will no more but abide.
4.3.86-87.

Your purse is not hot enough to purchase your spice.
4.3.114.

The gods themselves, humbling their deities to love, have taken the shapes of beasts upon them.
4.4.25-28.

Lift up your countenance, as it were the day
of celebration of that nuptial which
we two have sworn shall come.
4.4.49-51.

This is an art which does men nature-- change it rather; but the art itself is nature.
4.4.94-96.

Crowns what you are doing in the present deeds,
that all your acts are queens.
4.4.145-146.

This is the prettiest low-born lass that ever
ran on the green-sward; nothing she does or seems but smacks of something greater than herself,

too noble for this place.
4.4.156-158.

We stand upon our manners.
4.4.160.

There is not half a kiss to choose who loves another best.
4.4.175-176.

I love a ballad in print, for then we are sure they are true.
4.4.254.

Why should I carry lies abroad?
4.4.264.

By th' pattern of my own thoughts I cut out the purity of his.
4.4.373-374.

Thou art too base to be acknowleg'd.
4.4.411.

If I might die within this hour, I have liv'd
to die when I desire.
4.4.432.

It cannot fail but by the violation of my faith.
4.4.468-469.

If my reason
will thereto be obedient, I have reason;
if not, my senses better pleas'd with madness,
do bid it welcome.
4.4.474-476.

I am bound to you.
4.4.556.

As the unthought-on accident is guilty to what we wildly do, we profess ourselves to be the slaves of chance and flies of every wind that blows.
4.4.530-533.

Twixt his unkindness and his kindness- th'one
he chides to hell, and bids the other grow

faster than though or time.
4.4.544-547.

Besides, you know
Prosperity's the very bond of love,
Whose fresh complexion and whose heart together
Affliction alters.
4.4.564-566.

I think affliction may subdue the cheek,
but not take in the mind.
4.4.568.

What a fool honesty is! And trust, his sworn brother,
a very simple gentleman!
4.4.586-587.

This is the time that the unjust man doth thrive.
4.4.664.

Let me have no lying; it becomes none but tradesmen.
4.4.712.

All deaths are too few, the sharpest too easy.
4.4.769.

Though authority be a stubborn bear, yet it is oft led by the nose with gold.
4.4.789-790.

More penitence than done trespass.
5.1.4.

It is as bitter upon thy tongue as in my thought.
5.1.17-18.

Fear thou no wife .
5.1.68.

Infirmity, which waits upon worn times, hath something seiz'd
5.1.141-142.

The blessed gods purge all infection from our air whilst you do climate here!

5.1.168-171.

The stars... will kiss the valley first.
5.1.206.

If all the world could have seen it, the woe would have been universal.
5.2.88-89.

Our absence makes us unthrifty to our knowledge.
5.2.106-107.

What fine chisel could ever cut breath?
5.2.77-78.

Let no man mock me,
for I will kiss her.
5.2.79-80.

To see the life as lively knock'd as ever still sleep mocked death.
5.3.18-19.

Dear my brother,
Let him that was the cause of this have pow'r
To take off so much grief from you as he
Will piece up in himself.
5.3.53-56.

You do awake your faith. Then all stand still;
Or those that think it is unlawful business I am about, let them depart.
5.3.95-97.

If this be magic, let it be an art.
5.3.112.

PERICLES, PRINCE OF TYRE

To entice his own to evil should be done by none.
1.27-28.

Nature this dowry gave to glad her presence
1.1.9.

Here face the book of praises, where is read
nothing but curious pleasures
1.1.14-15.

Life's but breath.
1.1.46.

He's no man on whom perfections wait
that, knowing sin within, will touch the gate.
1.1.79-80.

Few love to hear the sins they love to act.
1.1.92.

The earth is throng'd by man's oppression,
and the poor worm doth die for't.
1.1.101-102.

The passions of the mind,
that have their first conception by misdread,
have after-nourishment and life by care
1.2.11-13.

They do abuse the king that flatter him .
1.2.38.

This thing the which is flatters is but a spark.
1.2.40.

He flatters you, makes war upon your life.
1.2.45.

Tis time to fear when tyrants kiss.
1.2.79.

Tyrants fears
decrease not, but grow faster than the years.
1.2.84-85.

For who digs hills because they do aspire
throws down one mountain to cast up a higher.
1.4.5-6.

So sharp are hunger's teeth that man and wife
draw lots who first shall die to lengthen life.
1.4.45-46.

One sorrow never comes but brings an heir
that may succeed as his inheritor.
1.4.63-64.

What I have been I have forgot to know;
but what I am want teaches me to think on.
2.1.71-72.

Beauty's child, whom nature gat
for men to see, and seeing wonder at.
2.2.6-7.

As jewels lose their glory if neglected,
so princes their renowns if not respected.
2.2.12-13.

Beauty hat his power and will,
which can as well inflame as it can kill.
2.2.34-35.

From the dejected state wherein he is,
he hopes by you his fortunes yet may flourish.
2.2.46-47.

Opinion's but a fool that makes us scan

the outward habit by the inward man
2.2.56-57.

We are gentlemen
that neither in our hearts nor outward eyes
envy the great nor shall the low despise.
2.3.24-26.

His greatness was no guard
to bar heaven's shaft, but sin had his reward.
2.4.14-15.

The best know how to rule and how to reign.
2.4.38.

To wisdom he's a fool that will not yield.
2.4.54.

My ears were never better fed
with such delightful pleasing harmony.
2.4.27-28.

My actions are as noble as my thoughts.
2.4.58.

O you gods!
Why do you make us love your goodly gifts,
and snatch them straight away?
3.1.22-24.

Virtue and cunning were endowments greater
than nobleness and riches.
3.2.27-28.

We cannot but obey
the powers above us.
3.3.9-10.

To you my good will is great, though the gift be small.
3.4.17.

I never kill'd a mouse, nor hurt a fly.
4.1.78-79.

If it please the gods to defend you by men, then men must comfort you, men must feed you, men must stir you up.
4.2.90-91.

You must seem to do that fearfully which you commit willingly; to despise profit where you have most to gain.
4.2.117-119.

Seldom but that pity begets you a good opinion.
4.2.121-122.

How belief may suffer by foul show!
4.4.23.

The fairest, sweetest, and best lies here,
who withered in her spring of year.
4.4.34-35.

She would make a puritan of the devil, if he should cheapen a kiss of her.
4.6.9-10.

This is the rarest dream that e'er dull sleep
did mock sad fools withal.
5.1.160-161.

Give me a gash, put me to present pain,
lest this great sea of joys rushing upon me
o'erbear the shores of my mortality.
5.1.189- 191.

It nips me unto list'ning, and this slumber
hangs upon mine eyes.
5.1.232-233.

Wishes fall out as they're will'd.
5.2.16.

The gods have no mortal officer
more like a god than you.
5.2.63-64.

Heavens make a star of him!

5.2.80.

THE TEMPEST

You mar our labour: keep your cabins; you do assist the storm.
1.1.15-160.

I'll warrant him for drowning; though the ship were no stronger than a nutshell and as leaky as an unstaunched wench.
1.1. 46-49

Now I would give a thousand furlongs of sea for an acre of barren ground, long heath, brown furze, any thing. The wills above be done! but I would fain die a dry death.
1.1.62-65

Your tale, sir, would cure deafness.
1.2.124

Good wombs have borne bad sons.
1.2.140

Hell is empty and all the devils are here.
1.2.247-8

Thou poisonous slave, got by the devil himself
upon thy wicked dam, come forth!
1.2.377-8

You taught me language, and my profit on't is, I know how to curse. The red plague rid you for learning me your language.
1.2.425-428

There's nothing ill can dwell in such a temple:
if the ill spirit have so fair a house,
Good things will strive to dwell with't.
1.2.533-535

My spirits, as in a dream, are all bound up.

1.2.573

Weigh our sorrow with our comfort.
2.1.9-10

He receives comfort like cold porridge.
2.1.12

You cram these words into my ears against the stomach of my sense.
2.1.99-100

O you, so perfect and so peerless, are created of every creatures' best!
3.1.45-47

I am a fool to weep at what I am glad of.
3.1.72

He that dies pays all debts!
3.2.126

Guilt, like poison given to work a great time after, now gins to bite the spirits.
3.2.104-105

The strongest oaths are straw to the fire in the blood.
4.1.52-53

We are such stuff as dreams are made on, and our little life is rounded with a sleep.
4.1.155-156

Let me embrace thine age, whose honour cannot be measur'd or confin'd.
5.1.120-121

There is in this business more than nature was ever conduct of.
5.1.242

What a thrice double ass was I to take this drunkard for a god, and worship this dull fool!
5.1.295-297

THE MERCHANT OF VENICE

In sooth, I know not why I am so sad.
1.1.1.

Shall I have the thought,
To think on this, and shall I lack the thought
That such a thing bechanc'd would make me sad?
1.1.35-37.

Your worth is very dear in my regard.
1.1.62.

You have too much respect upon the world; they lose it that do buy it with much care.
1.1.74-75.

I do know of these that therefore only are reputed wise for saying nothing.
1.1.94-96.

His reasons are as two grains of wheat hid in two bushels of chaff; you shall seek all day ere you find them, and when you have them they are not worth the search.
1.1.116-118.

The brain may devise laws for the blood, but a hot temper leaps o'er a cold decree.
1.2.16-17.

God made and therefore let him pass for a man.
1.2.50.

When he is best, he is little worse than a man, and when he is worst, he is little better than a beast.
1.2.76-77.

The man is, notwithstanding, sufficient.

1.3.23.

Why, look you how you storm!
I would be friends with you and have your love,
Forget the shames that you have stained me with,
Supply your present wants, and take no doit
Of usance for my moneys, and you'll not hear me!
This is kind I offer.
1.3.132-137.

What these Christians are,
whose own hard dealings teaches them suspect
the thoughts of others.
1.3.154-156.

You must take your chance.
2.1.38.

Well, if fortune be a woman, she's a good wench this year.
2.2.152.

Our house is hell and thou, a merry devil,
Didst rob it of some taste of tediousness.
2.3.2-3.

I am right loath to go;
There is some ill a-brewing towards my rest,
for I did dream of money-bags tonight.
2.5.16-18.

All things that are with more spirit chased than enjoyed.
2.6.12-13.

Not I, but my affairs, have made you wait.
2.6.21.

The pretty follies that themselves commit,
for, if they could, Cupid himself would blush
to see me thus transformed to a boy.
2.6.36-39.

All that glisters is not gold.
2.7.66.

O that estates, degrees, and offices
were not (delivered) corruptly, and that clear honour
were purchased by the merit of the wearer!
2.9.41-43.

How many be commanded with that command.
2.9.45.

To offend and judge are distinct offices
and of opposed natures.
2.9.61-62.

A maiden hath no tongue but thought.
3.2.8.

Prove it so,
Let fortune go to hell for it, not I.
3.2.19-20.

For as I am, I live upon the rack.
3.2.24.

The world is still deciev'd with ornament.
In law, what plea so tainted and corrupt
but being season'd with a gracious voice,
obscures the show of evil?
3.2.74-76.

There is no vice so simple but assumes
some mark of virtue on his outward parts.
3.2.81-82.

I wish you all the joy that you can wish.
3.2.191.

Never did I know
a creature that did bear the shape of man
so keen and greedy to confound a man.
3.2.276-277.

Thou calld'st me dog before thou hadst a cause,
but, since I am a dog, beware my fangs.

3.3.6-7.

I never did repent for doing good.
3.4.19.

The sins of the father are to be laid upon the children.
3.5.1-2.

Having such a blessing in his lady,
he finds the joys of heaven here on earth
3.5.66-67.

And by our holy sabbath have I sworn
To have the due and forfeit of my bond.
4.1.36-37.

Affection, mistress of passion, sways it to the mood of what it likes or loathes.
4.1.50-52.

Why he, a woollen bagpipe, but of force
must yield to such inevitable shame
as to offend, himself being offended.
4.1.56-59.

I am not bound to please thee with my answers.
4.1.65.

You may as well go stand upon the beach
And bid the main flood bate his usual height;
You may as well use question with the wolf
Why he hath made the ewe bleat for the lamb;
You may as well forbid the mountain pines
To wag their high tops and to make no noise,
When they are fretten with the gusts of heaven;
4.1.72-79.

How shalt thou hope for mercy, rendering none?
4.1.88.

The weakest kind of fruit drops earliest to the ground.
4.1.115.

O, be thou damned, inexecrable dog!
4.1.128.

The quality of mercy is not strain'd;
It droppeth as the gentle rain from heaven
upon the place beneath. It is twice best;
It blesseth him that gives and him that takes.
4.1.179-182.

Consider this—that in the course of justice none of us
Should see salvation; we do pray for mercy,
And that same prayer doeth teach us all to render
The deeds of mercy.
4.1.194-196.

Wrest once the law to your authority;
To do a great right to do a little wrong
and curb this cruel devil of his will.
4.1.210-212.

As thou urgest justice, be assur'd
thou shalt have justice, more than thou desir'st.
4.1.311-312.

You taught me first to beg, and now, methinks
You teach me ho a beggar should be answer'd.
4.1.434-435

When the moon shone, we did not see the candle.
so doth the greater glory dim the less;
5.1.92-93.

Give me light, but let me not be light,
for a light wife doth make a heavy husband.
5.1.129-130.

While I live, I'll fear no other thing
so sore as keeping safe Nerissa's ring.
5.1.306-307.

MEASURE FOR MEASURE

If our virtues did not go forth of use, twere all alike, as if we had then not.
1.1.34-35.

Grace is grace, despite of all controversy.
1.2.24

Impiety has made a feast of thee.
1.2.54.

Groping for trouts in a peculiar river.
1.2.86.

Good counsellors lack no clients.
1.2.101

I had as lief have the foppery of freedom as the morality of imprisonment. What's they offence, Claudio?
1.2.128.

The baby beats the nurse, and quite athwart goes all decorum.
2.3.29-31

Hence we shall see
if power change purpose, what our seemers be.
2.3.53-54

Our doubts are traitors, and make use lose the good we oft might win by fearing to attempt.
1.4.77-79

'Tis one thing to be tempted, Escalus, and another thing to fall.
2.1.16-17

What knows the laws that thieves do pass on thieves?

2.1.22-23

The jewel that we find, we stoop and take't,
because we see it; but what we do not see, we tread upon, and never think of it.
2.1.23-26

Some rise by sin, and some by virtue fall.
2.1.37

Authority, though it err like others,
Hath yet a kind of medicine in itself
That skins the vice o' th' top.
2.2.133-135.

The valiant heart's not whipped out of his trade.
2.2.241.

Mercy is not itself that oft looks so
pardon is still the nurse o woe.
2.2.268-270

Condemn the fault and not the actor of it!
2.3.38

That I will not, I cannot do.
2.3.53

It is the law, not I condemn your brother.
2.3.81

Shall we serve heaven with less respect than we do minister to our gross selves?
2.3.85-86

I show (pity) most of all when I show justice; for then I pity those I do no know.
2.3.99-101

O, it is excellent to have a giant's strength! But it is tyrannous to use it like a giant.
2.3.107-109

But man, proud man, dress'd in a little brief authority, most

ignorant of what he's most assur'd,s glass essence, like an angry ape, plays such fantastic tricks before high heaven as makes the angels weep; who, with our spleens, would laugh themselves mortal.
2.3.117-123

The tempter or the tempted, who sins most?
2.3.163

Most dangerous is that temptation that doth goad us on to sin in loving virtue.
2.3.181-182

Thus wisdom wishes to appear most bright
When it doth tax itself.
2.4.78-79

To have what we would have, we speak not what we mean; I something do excuse the thing I hate
for his advantage that I dearly love.
2.4.117-120

My false overweighs your true
2.4.170

If I do lose thee, I do lose a thing that none but fools would keep.
3.1.7-8

Merely, thou art death's fool;
For him thou labour'st by the flight o shun
And yet run'st toward him still.
3.1.11-13.

O, you beast!
O faithless coward! O dishonest wretch!
Wilt thou be made a man out of my vice?
3.1.137-139.

I am so out of love with life that I will sue to be rid of it.
3.1.170-171

Virtue is bold, and goodness never fearful.
3.1.203

There is scarce truth enough alive to make societies secure.
3.1.211-212

Love talks with better knowledge and knowledge with dearer love.
3.2.140.
When once our grace we have forgot, nothing goes right.
4.4.30-31

Do not banish reason for inequality, but let your reason serve to make the truth appear where it seems hid and hide the false seems true.
5.1.62-65

In this I'll be impartial; be you judge of your own cause.
5.1.166-167.

Haste still pays haste, and leisure answers leisure;
like doth quit like, and measure for measure.
5.1.408-409

Thoughts are no subjects; intents, but merely thoughts.
5.1.451-452

Your evil quits you well.
5.1.494

What's mine is yours and what's yours is mine.
5.1.535

THE TRAGEDIES

Technically, being the opposite of a comedy is all the qualification a play needs to be classified as a tragedy. Is the protagonist happy or does the play have a sad ending for them? That's a start but it wouldn't qualify it as a tragedy for most of us, and definitely not for high drama or Shakespearean tragedy.

Shakespeare leaps over the middle ground when he writes a tragedy. There is, in many cases, nothing left of the title character in a Shakespearean tragedy. They have ended miserably, they have ended painfully, and very often, they have ended completely. They are dead and miserably dead at that. To again quote Hamlet the true tragedy is that, "The cease of majesty dies not alone, but, like a gulf, doth draw what's near it with it". Whether it is majesty of station or majesty of character makes no difference. Capital "T" tragedies draw in everyone around the title character into a disappearing gulf of misery which offers no possible redemption for the chief protagonist and many of the supporting cast. That is high, dramatic, Shakespearean tragedy. Enjoy these quotes and do your best to avoid starring in your own tragedy. It would ruin not just your life but the lives of all those around you as well.

Order of the Tragedies:

Antony and Cleopatra
Coriolanus
Hamlet
King Lear
Macbeth
Othello
Julius Caesar
Romeo and Juliet
Timon of Athens
Titus Andronicus

ANTONY AND CLEOPATRA

I love long life better than figs.
1.2.31.

Kingdoms are clay; our dungy earth alike feeds beast and man.
1.2.34-35.

Be more loving than beloved.
1.2.22.

What our contempts doth often hurt from us we wish it ours again; the present pleasure, by revolution low'ring, does become the opposite of itself.
1.2.120-123.

My full heart remains in use with you.
1.3.43-44.

Though age from folly could not give me freedom, it does from childishness.
1.3.57-58.

You shall find there
A man who is the abstract of all faults
That all men follow.
1.3.79.

This common body,
like to a vagabond flag upon the stream,
goes to and back, lackeying the varying tide,
to rot itself with motion.
1.4.44-47.

Now I feed myself
Withy most delicious poison.
1.5.26-27.

If the great gods be just, they shall assist the deeds of justest men.
2.1.1-2.

When we debate our trivial difference loud, we do commit murder in healing wounds.
2.2.20-22.

Would we had all such wives, that the men might go to wars with the women!
2.2.69-70.

May I never to this good purpose, that so fairly shows, dream of impediment!
2.2.148-150.
It beggar'd all description.
2.2.202.

Royal wench!
She made great Caesar lay his royal sword to bed.
He ploughed her, and she cropp'd.
2.2.230-232.

No worse a husband than the best of men;
Whose virtue and whose general graces speak
That which none else can utter. By this marriage
All little jealousies, which now seem great,
And all great fears, which now import their dangers,
Would then be nothing. Truths would be tales,
Where now half tales be truths.
2.2.133-139.

Age cannot wither her, nor custom stale her infinite variety. Other women cloy the appetites they feed, but she makes hungry where most she satisfies.
2.2.249-242.

If thou dost play with him at any game, thou are sure to lose; and of that natural luck he beats thee 'gainst the odds.
2.3.26-28.

Music, moody food, of us that trade in love.
2.5.1-2.

I do no like 'but yet'. It does allay the good precedence; fie upon 'but yet'!
'But yet' is as a gaoler to bring forth some monstrous malefactor.
2.5.50-53.

I that do bring the news made not the match.
2.5.68.

Some innocents 'scape not the thunderbolt.
2.5.77.

These hands do lack nobility, that they strike a meaner than myself, since I myself have given myself the cause.
2.5.82-84.

Though it be honest, it is never good to bring bad news.
2.5.85-86.

I never hated thee; I have seen thee fight, when I have envied thy behaviour.
2.6.73-74.

All men's faces are true, whatsoe'er their hands are but there is never a fair woman that has a true face.
2.6.97-98.

The band that seems to tie their friendship together will be the very strangler of their amity.
2.6.117-118.

It's monstrous labour when I wash my brain
And it grows fouler.
2.7.98-99.

Better to leave undone than by our deed acquire too high a fame when him we serve's away. Caesar and Antony have ever won more in their officer, than person.
3.1.14-17.

You take from me a great part of myself.

3.1.24.

Women are not in their best fortune's strong; but want will perjure the ne'er touch'd vestal.
3.12.29-31.

Her heart will not obey her tongue, nor can her heart inform her tongue.
3.2.48.

If I love mine honour,
I lose myself.
3.4.22-23.

Ay me most wretched,
that have my heart parted betwixt two friends,
that does afflict each other!
3.6.77-79.

Cheer your heart;
Be you not troubled with the time, which drives
O'er your contest these strong necessities,
But let determin'd things go to destiny
Hold unbewail'd their way.
3.6.81-83.

I never saw an action of such shame.
3.9.22.

Think, and die.
3.13.2.

Mine honour was not yielded, but conquer'd merely.
3.13.61.

'Tis your noblest course.
Wisdom and fortune combating together,
if that the former dare but what it can,
n chance may shake it.
3.13.78-81.

'Tis better to play with a lion's whelp than with an old dying one.
3.13.93-94.

When we in our viciousness grow hard...
the wise gods seal our eyes,
in our own filth drop our clear judgments, make us
adore our errors, laugh at's while we strut
to our confusion.
3.13.111-114.

For when our hours were nice and lucky, men did ransom lives of
me for jests; but now I'll set my teeth,
and send to darkness all that stop me.
3.13.179-182.

Let's mock the midnight bell.
3.13.184.

Transform us not to women.
4.2.31.

Let's go to supper, come,
and drown consideration.
4.2.44-45.

Thou art the armorer of my heart.
4.4.6-7.

To business that we love we rise betimes,
and go to't with delight.
4.4.20-21.

O, my fortunes have corrupted honest men!
4.5.16-17.

I am alone the villain of the earth,
and feel I am so most.
4.6.30-31.

This blows my heart.
If swift thought break it not, a swifter mean
Shall outstrike thought; but thought will do't, I feel.
4.6.34-36.

I will go seek some ditch wherein to die;

the foulest best fits my latter part of life.
4.6.37-39.

O thou day o' th' world, chain mine arm'd neck.
Leap thou, attire and all, through proof of harness to my heart, and there ride on the pants triumphing.
4.8.14-16.

Though grey do something mingle with our younger brown, yet ha' we a brain that nourishes our nerves, and can get goal for goal of youth.
4.8.20-23.

That thou depart'st hence safe does pay thy labour nicely.
4.14.36-37.

I have liv'd in such dishonour that the gods detest my baseness.
4.14.56-57.

With a wound I must be cur'd
4.14.78.

Bid that welcome which comes to punish us, and we punish it, seeming to bear it lightly.
4.14.136-138.

So it should be, that none but Antony
should conquer Antony.
4.15.16-17.

The miserable change now at my end
lament nor sorrow at; but please your thoughts
in feeding them with those my former fortunes
wherein I liv'd the greatest prince o' th' world,
the noblest; and do now not basely die,
not cowardly put off my helmet to
my countryman-- a Roman by a Roman
valiantly vanquish'd.
4.15.51-58.

Hast thou no care of me? Shall I abide
in this dull world, which in thy absence is

no better than a sty? O, see, my women,
the crown o' th' earth doeth melt.
4.15.59-62.

The breaking of so great a thing should make a greater crack.
5.1.14-15.

Strange it is that nature must compel us to lament our most persisted deeds.
5.1.28-30.

A rarer spirit never did steer humanity.
5.1.31-32.

When such a spacious mirror's set before him,
he needs must see himself.
5.1.33-34.

This mortal house I'll ruin, do Caesar what he can.
5.2.51-52.

Take to you no hard thoughts.
The record of what injuries you did us, though written in our flesh, we shall remember as things but done by chance.
5.2.116-119.

Wert thou a man
thou wouldst have mercy on me.
5.2.173-174.

We, the greatest, are misthought
for things that others do; and when we fall
we answer others' merits in our name,
5.2.173-175.

What poor an instrument may do a noble deed!
5.2.235-236.

He that will believe all that they say shall never be saved by half that they do.
5.2.254-255.

The stroke of death is as a lover's pinch,

which hurts and is desir'd.
5.2.292-293.

High events as these strike those that make them, and their story is no less in pity than his glory which brought them to be lamented.
5.2.356-360.

CORIOLANUS

The leanness that afflicts us, the object of our misery, is an inventory to particularize their abundance; our sufferance is a gain to them.
1.1.16-18.

You may as well strike at the heaven with your staves as lift them against the Roman state.
1.1.63-65.

Though all at once cannot see what I do deliver out to each, yet I can make my audit up, that all from me do back receive the flour of all, and leave me but the bran.
1.1.140-144.

What would you have, you curs,
that like not peace nor war?
1.1.167-168.

He that trusts to you, where he should find you lions, finds you hares; where foxes, geese; you are no surer, non
than is the coals of fire upon the ice or hailstone in the sun. Your virtues is to make him worthy whose offences subdues him, and curse that justice did it. Who deserves greatness deserves your hate; and your affections are
a sicks man's appetite, who desires most that which would increase his evil.
1.1.165-177.

He is a lion that I am proud to hunt.
1.1.233-234.

I had rather had eleven die nobly for their country than one voluptuously surfeit out of action.
1.3.24-25.

He had rather see the sword and hear a drum than look upon his schoolmaster.
1.3.55-56.

Now put your shields before your hearts, and fight
with hearts more proof than shields.
1.4.24-25.

You souls of geese
that bear the shapes of men, how have you run
from slaves that apes would beat!
1.4.34-36.

Though thou speak'st truth,
methinks thou speak'st not well.
1.6.13-14.

The shepherd knows not thunder from a tabor.
1.6.25.

If any think brave death outweighs bad life
and that his country's dearer than himself,
let him alone.
1.6.71-72.

You shall not be the grave of your own deserving.
1.9.19-20.

What good condition can a treaty find
i' th' part that is at mercy?
1.10.6-7.

Nature teaches beasts how to know their friends.
2.1.5.

A very little thief of occasion will rob you of a great deal of patience.
2.1.26-27.

Death, that dark spirit, in's nervy arm doth lie,
Which, being advanc'd, declines, and then men must die.
2.1.151-152.

Our veil'd dames
Commit the war of white and damask in
Their nicely gawded cheeks to th' wanton spoil
Of Phoebus' burning kisses.
2.1.205-208.

Doubt not the commoners, for whom we stand, but they upon their ancient malice will forget with the least cause these his new honours.
2.1.217-220.

Faith, there have been many great men that have flatter'd the people, who ne'er loved them.
2.2.7-8.

Now to seem to affect the malice and displeasure of the people is as bad as that which he dislikes- to flatter them for their love.
2.2.20-22.

It is held that valour is the chiefest virtue and
most dignifies man.
2.2.81-83.

He cannot but with measure fit the honours
which we devise him.
2.2.121-122.

Ingratitude is monstrous, and for the multitude to be ingrateful were to make a monster of the multitude; of the which we being members should bring ourselves to be monstrous members.
2.3.10-13.

Better it is to die, better to starve
Than crave the hire which first we do deserve.
Why in this wolvish toge should I stand here
To beg of Hob and Dick that do appear
Their needless vouches?
2.3.110-115.

Did you perceive
He did solicit you in free contempt

When he did need your loves, and do you think
That his contempt shall not be bruising to you
When he hath power to crush? Why, had your bodies
No heart among you? Or had you tongues to cry
Against the rectorship of judgment?
2.3.196-213.

They have chose a consul that will from them take
their liberties, make them of not more voice
than dogs, that are as often beat for barking
as therefore kept to do so.
2.3.211-214.

Bid them wash their faces
And keep their cheeks clean.
2.4.59-60.

You should account me the more virtuous, that I have not been common in my love.
2.4.91-92.

He would pawn his fortunes to hopeless restitution, so he might be call'd your vanquisher.
3.1.15-17.

As I live, I will.
3.1.64.

You speak o' th' people as if you were a god, to punish;
not a man of their infirmity.
3.1.80-82.

Manhood is call'd foolery when it stands against a falling fabric.
3.1.246-247.

The service of the foot, being once gangren'd, is not then respected for what before it was.
3.1.306-308.

You might have been enough the man you are with striving less to be so.

3.2.18-19.

I have a heart as little apt as yours,
but yet a brain that leads my use of anger
to better vantage.
3.2.28-30.

Honour and policy, like unsever'd friends,
i' th' war do grow together.
3.2.42-43.

Action is eloquence, and the eyes of th' ignorant
more learned than the ears
3.2.76-77.

Prithee now,
Go, and be ruled; although I know thou hadst rather
Follow thine enemy in a fiery gulf
Than flatter him in a bower.
3.2.89-92.

I will not do't,
lest I surcease to honour mine own truth,
and by my body's action teach my mind
a most inherent baseness.
3.2.120-123.

There's no more to be said, but he is banished
 As enemy to the people and his country.
 It shall be so.
3.3.118-120.

There is a world elsewhere.
3.3.136.

Extremities ... the trier of spirits;
... common chances common men could bear
4.1.4-5.

When the sea was calm all boats alike show'd mastership in floating.

4.1.6-7.

I shall be lov'd when I am lack'd.
4.1.15.

I sup upon myself;
And so shall starve with feeding.
4.1.50-51.

The fittest man to corrupt a man's wife is when she's fall'n out with her husband.
4.3.28-30.

O world, thy slippery turns!
4.4.12.

He is simply the rarest man i' th' world.
4.5.160-161.

War... it exceeds peace as far as day does night.
4.5.221-222.

The present peace and quietness of the people, which before were in a wild hurry, here do make his friends blush that he world goes well.
4.6.2-5.

That we did, we did for the best.
4.6.145.

I must excuse what cannot be amended.
4.7.11-12.

Power, unto itself commendable, hath not a tomb so evident as a chair t' extol what it hath done.
4.7.51-53.

Rights by rights falter, strengths by strengths do fail.
4.7.54.

I melt, and am not of stronger earth than others.
5.3.29-30.

Like a dull actor now I have forgot my part and I am out,

even to a full disgrace.
5.3.40-42.

There is no more mercy in him than milk in a male tiger.
5.5.27-28.

HAMLET, PRINCE OF DENMARK

It started like a guilty thing upon a fearful summons
1.1.148-149.

All that lives must die, passing through nature to eternity.
1.2.72-73.

I know not seems.
1.2.76.

To persevere in obstinate condolement is a course of impious stubbornness.
1.2.92-94.

Tis unmanly grief;
it shows a will most incorrect to heaven
1.2.95-96.

Tis a fault to heaven
A fault against the dead, a fault to nature,
to reason most absurd;
1.2.101-103.

O, that this too, too, solid flesh would melt
Thaw, and resolve itself into a dew!
1.2.129-130.

'tis an unweeded garden, that grows to seed;
things rank and gross in nature possess it merely.
1.2.135-137.

As if increase of appetite had grown by what it fed on
1.2.143-144.

Was a man, take him for all in all,
I shall not look upon his like again.

1.2.187-188.

All is not well. I doubt some foul play.
1.2.254-255.

Foul deeds will rise,
though all the earth o'erwhelm them, to men's eyes.
1.2.256-257.

His greatness weigh'd, his will is not his own.
1.3.17.

Keep you in the rear of your affection,
out of the shot and danger of desire.
1.3.34-35.

The chariest maid is prodigal enough
if she unmask her beauty to the moon.
1.3.36-37.

Virtue itself scapes not calumnious strokes.
1.3.38.

Best safety lies in fear.
1.3.43.

Youth to itself rebels.
1.3.44.

But, good my brother,
Do not, as some ungracious pastors do,
Show me the steep and thorny way to heaven,
Whiles, ⟨like⟩ a puffed and reckless libertine,
Himself the primrose path of dalliance treads
and recks not his own rede.
1.3.50-56.

Those friends thou hast, and heir adoption tried,
Grapple them to thy soul with hoops of steel
1.3.62-63.

Beware of entrance to a quarrel; but, being in,
bear't that th' opposed may beware of thee.

1.3.65-67.

The apparel oft proclaims the man.
1.3.72.

Neither a borrower nor a lender be'
for loan oft loses both itself and friend,
and borrowing dulls the edge of husbandry.
1.3.75-77.

This above all- to thine own self be true,
and it must follow, as the night the day,
thou canst not then be false to any man.
1.3.78-80.

Tender yourself more dearly, or... you'll tender me a fool.
1.3.107-109.

When the blood burns, how prodigal the soul
lends the tongue vows.
1.3.116-117.

It is a custom
More honour'd in the breach than in the observance.
1.4.15-16.

Nature cannot choose his origin.
1.4.25.

Angels and ministers of grace defend us!
1.4.38.

I do not set my life at a pin's fee.
1.4.65.

My fate cries out,
And makes each petty arture in this body
as hardy as the nemean lion's nerve.
1.4.81-83.

Murder most foul, as in the best it is
1.4.27.

The serpent that did sting thy father's life

now wears his crown.
1.4.39-40.

There are more things in heaven and earth, Horatio,
Than are dreamt of in your philosophy.
1.4.166-167.
Revenge his foul and most unnatural murder.
1.5.25.

The time is out of joint. O cursed spite,
That ever I was born to set it right.
1.5.189-190.

Such wanton, wild, and usual slips
as are companions noted and most known
to youth and liberty.
2.1.22-24.

By heaven, it is as proper to our age
to cast beyond ourselves in our opinions
As it is common for the younger sort
to lack discretion.
2.1.114-117.

Something is rotten in the state of Denmark.
2.4.89.

Doubt thou the stars are fire;
Doubt that the sun doth move;
Doubt truth to be a liar;
But never doubt I love.
2.2.115-118.

To be honest, as this world goes, is to be one man pick'd out of ten thousand.
2.2.177-178.

Though this be madness, yet there is method in't.
2.2.204.

There is nothing either good or bad, but thinking makes it so.
2.2.248-249.

I could be bounded in a nutshell and count myself a
king of infinite space, were it not that I have bad dreams.
2.2.254-255.

What a piece of work is man!
2.2.303-304.

Man delights not me-- no, nor woman neither, though by your smiling you seem to say so.
2.2.308-309.

An old man is twice a child.
2.2.380.

An excellent play, well digested in the scenes, set down with as much modesty as cunning.
2.2.432-433.

They are the abstract and brief chronicles of the time.
2.2.517-518.

Use every man after his desert, and who shall scape the whipping?
2.2.522-523.

Use them after your own honour and dignity; the less they deserve, the more merit is in your bounty.
2.2.525-526.

O, what a rogue and peasant slave am I!
2.2.542.

The play's the thing,
wherein I'll catch the conscience of the King.
2.2.600-601.

With devotion's visage and pious action we do sugar o'er the devil himself.
3.1.247-249.

To be or not to be-- that is the question.
3.1.56.

To die to sleep-
no more; and by a sleep to say we end
the heart-ache and the thousand natural shocks
that flesh is heir to.
3.1.60-63.

Who would these fardels bear,
to grunt and sweat under a weary life,
but that the dread of something after death—
the undiscover'd country, from whose bourn
no traveller returns-- puzzles the will,
and makes us rather bear those ills we have
than fly to others that we know not of?
Thus conscience does make cowards of us all.
3.1.76-83.

Rich gifts wax poor when givers prove unkind.
3.1.100-101.

Your honesty should admit no discourse to your beauty.
3.1.106-107.

If thou wilt needs marry, marry a fool; for wise men know well
enough what monsters you make of them.
3.1.137-139.

God hath given you one face, and you make yourselves another.
3.1.142-143.

O, woe is me T' have seen what I have seen, see what I see!
3.1.160-161.

Madness in great ones must not unwatch'd go.
3.1.188.

O, it offends me to the soul to hear a robustious periwig pated
fellow tear a passion to tatters, to very rags, to split the ears of the
groundlings, who, for the most part, are capable of nothing but
inexplicable dumb shows and noise.
3.2.8-12.

Let your own discretion be your tutor.
3.2.16.

Suit the action to the word, the word to the action.
3.2.18.

I have thought some of Nature's journeymen had made men, and not made them well, they imitated humanity so abominably.
3.2.32-34.

Why should the poor be flatter'd?
3.2.57.

Give me that man that is not passion's slave, and I will wear him in my heart's core, ay, in my heart of hearts, as I do thee.
3.2.69-72.

It was a brute part of him to kill so capital a calf there.
3.2.101.

What should a man do but be merry?
3.2.120-121.

O heavens! Die two months ago, and not forgotten yet? Then there's hope a great man's memory may outlive his life half a year.
3.2.126-128.

For women fear too much even as thy love,
And women's fear and love hold quantity,
In neither aught, or in extremity.
Where loves is great, the littlest doubts are fear;
Where little fears grow great, great love grows there.
3.2.165-168.

But what we do determine oft we break.
3.2.182.

Purpose is but the slave to memory,
of violent birth, but poor validity.
3.2.184-185.

'Tis not strange

That even our loves should with our fortunes change
3.2.196-197.

Love lead fortune or else fortune love.
3.2.198.

The lady doth protest too much, methinks.
3.2.225.

Frighted with false fire
3.2.260.

Why, look you now, how unworthy a thing you make of me! You would play upon me; you would seem to know my stops; you would pluck out the heart of my mystery; you would sound me from my lowest note to the top of my compass: and there is much music, excellent voice, in this little organ; yet cannot you make it speak. 'Sblood, do you think I am easier to be played on than a pipe? Call me what instrument you will, though you can fret me, yet you cannot play upon me.
3.2.353-363.

Now could I drink hot blood,
and do such bitter business as the day
would quake to look on.
3.2.380-383.

The cease of majesty dies not alone, but like a gulf doth draw what's near it with it.
3.3.15-17.

Never alone
Did the king sigh, but with a general groan.
3.3.22-23.
My stronger guilt defeats my strong intent,
And, like a man to double business bound,
I stand in pause where I shall first begin
And both neglect. What if this cursèd hand
Were thicker than itself with brother's blood?

3.3.40-44.

Whereto serves mercy but to confront the visage of offence?
3.3.46-47.

Oft tis seen the wicked prize itself buys out the law.
3.3.59-60.

Words without thoughts never to heaven go.
3.3.98.

Conceit in weakest bodies strongest works.
3.4.113.

I must be cruel to be kind.
3.4.178.

For 'tis the sport to have the engineer
Hoist with his own petar.
3.4.206-207.

O, 'tis most sweet
when in one line two crafts directly meet.
3.4.209-210.

How shall this bloody deed be answered?
4.1.16.

How all occasions do inform against me
And spur my dull revenge. What is a man
If his chief good and market of his time
Be but to sleep and feed? A beast, no more.
Sure He that made us with such large discourse,
Looking before and after, gave us not
That capability and godlike reason
To fust in us unused.
4.4.34-41.

Where th' offence is, let the great axe fall.
I pray you go with me.
4.4.216.

So full of artless jealousy is my guilt,
it spills itself in fearing to be split.
4.5.19-20.

When sorrows come, they come not single spies,
but in battalions!
4.5.75-76.

O heavens! is't possible a young maid's wits
should be as mortal as an old man's life?
4.5.157-158.

You must not think that we are made of stuff so flat and dull that
we can let our beard be shook with danger, and think it pastime.
4.7.30-33.

Know that love is begun by time.
4.7.111.

There lives within the very flame of love
A kind of wick or snuff that will abate it;
And nothing is at a like goodness still;
For goodness, growing to a pleurisy,
Dies in his own too much.
4.7.114-118.

That we would do, we should do when we would; for this 'would'
changes, and hath abatements and delays as many as there are
tongues, are hands, are accidents;
and then this 'should' is like a spendthrift's sigh, that hurts by
easing.
4.7.118-123.

Revenge should have no bounds.
4.7.128.

One woe doth tread upon another's heel, so fast they follow.
4.7.164-165.

Nature her custom holds, let shame say what it will.
4.7.188-189.

An act hath three branches- it is to act, to do, to perform.
5.1.12.

He that is not guilty of his own death shortens not his own life.
5.1.20.

The hand of little employment hath the daintier sense.
5.1.69-70.

We must speak by the card, or equivocation will undo us.
5.1.132-133.

Alas, poor Yorick! I knew him, Horatio: a fellow
of infinite jest, of most excellent fancy: he hath
borne me on his back a thousand times; and now, how
abhorred in my imagination it is! my gorge rims at
it. Here hung those lips that I have kissed I know
not how oft. Where be your gibes now? your
gambols? your songs? your flashes of merriment,
that were wont to set the table on a roar? Not one
now, to mock your own grinning? quite chap-fallen?
Now get you to my lady's chamber, and tell her, let
her paint an inch thick, to this favour she must
come; make her laugh at that. Prithee, Horatio, tell
me one thing.
5.1.178-190.

To what base uses we may return
5.1.197.

Why may not the imagination trace the noble dust of Alexander
till 'a find it stopping a bung-hole?
5.1.198-199.

'Twere to consider too curiously to consider it.
5.1.200.

Sweets to the sweet,
5.1.237.

Our indiscretion sometimes serves us well, when our deep plots

do pall; and that should learn us. There's a divinity that shapes
our ends, rough-hew them as we will.
5.2.8-11.

Tis dangerous when the baser nature comes
between the pass and fell incensed points
of mighty opposite.
5.2.60-62.

Let a beast be lord of beasts.
5.2.86.

I am constant to my purposes.
5.2.193.

Not a whit, we defy augury: there's a special
providence in the fall of a sparrow. If it be now,
'tis not to come; if it be not to come, it will be
now; if it be not now, yet it will come: the
readiness is all: since no man has aught of what he
leaves, what is't to leave betimes? Let be.
5.2.208-210.

Was't Hamlet wrong'd Laertes? Never Hamlet.
If Hamlet from himself be ta'en away,
and when he's not himself, does wrong Laertes,
then Hamlet does it not, Hamlet denies it.
Who does it, then? His madness.
5.2.225-229.

I am justly kill'd with mine own treachery.
5.2.299.

The foul practice hath turn'd itself on me.
5.2.309-310.

Here, thou incestuous, murd'rous, damned Dane,
Drink off this potion. Is thy union here?
Follow my mother!
5.2.315-318.

Horatio, I am dead: thou livest;

report me and my cause aright to the unsatisfied.
5.2.330-332.

Good night, sweet prince,
And flights of Angels sing thee to thy rest!
5.2.351-352.

Such a sight as this becomes the field,
but here shows much amiss.
5.2.393-394.

KING LEAR

Nothing will come of nothing; speak again.
1.1.90.

Think'st thou that duty shall have dread to speak
when power to flattery bows?
1.1.146-147.

Nor are those empty-hearted whose low sounds
reverb no hollowness.
1.1.152-153.

Love's not love
When it is mingled with regards that stands
Aloof from th' entire point. Will you have her?
She is herself a dowry.
1.1.238-241.

I think the world's asleep.
1.3.46.

Turn all her mother's pains and benefits
To laughter and contempt, that she may feel
How sharper than a serpent's tooth it is
To have a thankless child.
1.4.286-289.

Thou shouldn't not have been old till thou hadst been wise.
1.5.41.

Keep me in temper; I would not be mad!
1.5.43.

Thou whoreson zed!
2.2.59.

Noting almost sees miracles but misery.
2.2.160-161.

We are not ourselves
When nature, being oppress'd, commands the mind
To suffer with the body.
2.4.105-107.

Fortune, that arrant whore, ne'er turns the key to th' poor.
2.4.51-52.

O, reason not the need! Our basest beggars
are in the poorest thing superfluous.
2.4.263-264.

I tax not you, you elements, with unkindness;
I never gave you kingdom, call'd you children;
You owe me no subscription.
3.2.16-18.

Things that love night
love not such nights as these.
3.2.42-43.

I am a man
More sinn'd against than sinning.
3.2.58-59.

The art of our necessities is strange
That can make vile things precious.
3.2.70-71.

The younger rises, when the old doth fall.
3.3.25.

When the mind's free the body's delicate.
3.4.11-12.

The prince of darkness is a gentleman
3.4.139.

How malicious is my fortune, that I must repent to be just!
3.5.8.

He's mad that rust in the tameness of a wolf, a horse's
Health, a boy's love, or a whore's oath.
3.6.18-19.

When we our betters see bearing our woes,
We scarcely think our miseries our foes.
3.6.102-103.

Let is see more, prevent it! Out vile jelly!
Where is thy luster now?
3.7.82-83.

Out vile jelly!
Where is thy lustre now?
3.7.82-83.

World, world, O world!
But that thy strange mutations make us hate thee,
life would not yield to age.
4.1.10-12.

As flies to wanton boys are we to the gods-
they kill us for their sport.
4.1.36-37.

You are not worth the dust which the rude wind
blows in your face.
4.2.30-31.

Filths savour but themselves.
4.2.38.

If that the heavens do not their visible spirits
send quickly down to tame these vile offences,
it will come
humanity must perforce prey on itself,
like monsters of the deep.

4.2.46-49.

Proper deformity shows not in the fiend
so horrid as in woman
4.2.60-61.

O you mighty gods!
This world I do renounce, and in your sights
shake patiently my great affliction off
4.6.34-36.

How conceit may rob
the treasury of life, when life itself
yields to the theft.
4.6.42-44.

'Twas yet some comfort,
when misery could beguile the tyrant's rage
and frustrate his proud will.
4.6.62-64.

Bear free and patient thoughts.
4.6.79.

Nature's above art.
4.6.86.

Ay, every inch a king.
4.6.107.

O ruin'd piece of nature! This great world
shall so wear out to nought.
4.6.134-135.

A man may see how this world goes with no eyes. Look with thine ears.
4.6.150-151.

Thou might'st behold the great image of authority; a dog's obey'd in office.
4.6.158-159.

Get thee glass eyes,

and, like a scurvy politician, seem
to see the things thou dost not.
4.6.170-172.

Reason in madness!
4.6.176.

Thou must be patient; we came crying hither.
Thou know'st the first time that we smell the air
we wawl and cry.
4.6.179-181.

When we are born, we cry that we are come to this great age of
fools.
4.6.184-185.

I am bound
upon a wheel of fire, that mine own tears
do scald like molten lead.
4.7.46-48.

If you have poison for me, I will drink it.
4.7.73.

If you have poison for me I will drink it;
I know you do not love me; for your sisters
Have, as I do remember, done me wrong;
You have some cause, they have not.
4.8.72-74.

Know thou this, that men are as the time is;
to be tender-minded does not become a sword.
5.3.31-33.

The gods are just, an our pleasant vices
Make instruments to plague us
5.3.170-171.

The wheel's come full circle.
5.3.174.

I was contracted to them both;
All three are wedded in an instant.
5.3.228-229.

Howl, howl, howl! O, you are men of stones!
Had I your tongues and eyes, I'd use them so That heaven's vault should crack. She's gone
forever. I know when one is dead and when one lives.
She's dead as earth.—Lend me a looking glass.
If that her breath will mist or stain the stone, Why, then she lives.
5.3.257-262.

He hates him that would upon the rack of this tough world stretch him out longer.
5.3.312-314.

The weight of this sad time we must obey;
speak what we feel, not what we ought to say.
5.3.323-324.

The oldest hath borne most; we that are young
shall never see so much nor live so long.
5.3.325-326.

MACBETH

Fair is foul, and foul is fair
Hover through the fog and the filthy air.
1.1.10-11.

The multiplying villainies of nature
Do swarm upon him.
1.2.11-12.

He unseeme'd im from the navel to chaps
1.2.22.

Present fears are less than horrible imaginings.
1.3.137-138.

What? Can the devil speak true?
1.3.107.

If chance will have me king, why, chance may crown me.
1.3.154-144.

Come what come may,
time and hour runs through the roughest day.
1.3.146-147.

Nothing in his life became him like the leaving it.
1.4.7-8.

There's no art to find the mind's construction in the face.
1.4.11-13.

More is due than more than all can pay.
1.4.21

Let not light see my black and deep desires.
1.4.51.

Unsex me here,
and fill me from the crown to the toe top full of direst cruelty.
1.5.40 – 43.

To beguile the time look like the time; bear welcome in your eye,
your hand, your tongue; look like the innocent flower.
But be the serpent under't.
1.5.62-65.

This castle hath a pleasing seat; the air nimbly and sweetly recommends itself unto our gentle senses.
Macbeth; 1.6.1-3.

If it were done when 'tis done, then 'twere well it were done quickly.
1.7.1-2.

We still have judgment here; that we but teach bloody instructions, which, being taught, return to plague the inventor.
1.7.8-10.

I have no spur
To prick the sides of my intent, but only
Vaulting ambition, which o'erleaps itself,
And falls on th' other.
1.7.25-28.

I dare do all that may become a man;
who dares do more is none.
1.7.45-46.

If we should fail... we fail, but screw your courage to the sticking-place, and we'll not fail.
1.7.58-60.

False face must hide what the false heart doth know.
1.7.82.

Is this a dagger which I see before me,
The handle toward my hand? Come, let me clutch thee.
2.1.33-35.

Thou sure and firm-set earth,
hear not my steps, which way they walk, for fear
thy very stones prate of my whereabouts.
2.1.56-57.

That which hath made them drunk hath made me bold.
2.2.1.

Had he not resembled my father as he slept, I had done't.
2.2.13-14.

I am afraid to think what I have done;
Look on't again I dare not.
2.2.52-53.

'tis the eye of childhood that fears a painted devil.
2.2.54-55.

Will all great Neptunes' ocean wash this blood clean from my hand? No, this my hand will rather the multitudinous seas incarnadine.
2.2.60-63.

A little water clears us of this deed.
2.2.67.

Lechery, sir, it provokes and unprovokes. It provokes the desire, but it takes away the performance.
2.3.26-27.

Tongue nor heart cannot conceive nor name thee!
2.3.65-66.

The expedition of my violent love outran the pauser, my reason.
2.3.114-115.

Why do we hold our tongues that most claim this argument for ours?
2.3.123-124.

To show an unfelt sorrow is an office which the false man does easy.
2.3.123-124.

Where we are, there's daggers in men's smiles:
The nearer in blood, the nearer bloody.
2.3.144-145.

I am one, my liege, whom the vile blows and buffets of the world have so incens'd that I am reckless what I do to spite the world.
3.1.108-110.

Things without all remedy should be without regard; what's done is done.
3.2.10-12.

Better be with the dead, whom we, to gain our peace, have sent to peace than on the torture of the mind to live in restless ecstasy.
3.2.18-21.

O! Full of scorpions is my mind, dear wife.
3.2.36.

Thou canst not say I did it; never shake they gory locks at me.
3.4.50-51.

Things had begun to make strong themselves by ill.
3.2.55.

If I stand here, I saw him.
3.4.75.

Double, double, toil and trouble;
Fire burn and cauldron bubble.
4.1.10-11.

By the pricking of my thumbs, something wicked this way comes.
4.1.44.

Who can impress the forest, bid the tree unfix his earth bound root?
4.1.95-96.

When our actions do not, our fears do make us traitors.
4.2.3-4.

But cruel are the times when we are traitors and do not know ourselves, when we hold spea from what we fear, yet know not what we fear.
4.2.18-21.

There are liars and swearers enow to beat the honest men and hang them up.
4.2.53-55.

But I remember now I am in this earthly world, where to do harm is often laudable, to do good sometime accounted dangerous folly.
4.2.72-75.

Boundless intemperance in nature is tyranny. It hath been th' untimely emptying of the happy throne, and all of many kings.
4.3.66-69.

Let's make medicine of our great revenge, to cure this deadly grief.
4.3.14-17.

Your castle is surpris'd; your wife and babes
Savagely slaughter'd.
4.3.205.

Dispute it like a man.
4.3.218.

I shall do so; but I must also feel it like a man.
4.3.190.

The night is long that never finds the day.
4.3.239.

All the perfumes of Arabia will not sweeten this little hand.
5.1.48-49.

To-morrow and to-morrow and to-morrow,
creeps in this petty pace from day to day
to the last syllable of recorded time,

and all our yesterdays have lighted fools
the way to dusty death. Out, out, brief candle!
Life's but a walking shadow, a poor player,
that struts and frets his hour upon the stage,
and then is heard no more; it is a tale
told by an idiot, full of sound and fury,
signifying nothing.
5.5.19-28.

They have tied me to a stake; I cannot fly, but bear-like must fight the course.
5.7.1-2.

OTHELLO

I know my price, I am worth no worse a place.
1.1.12.

I would rather have been his hangman.
1.1.34.

Heaven is my judge.
1.1.60.

The beast with two backs .
1.1.116.

Fathers, from hence trust not your daughters' minds
By what you see them act.
1.170-171.

My parts, my title, and my perfect soul shall manifest me rightly.
1.2.31-32.

Men do their broken weapons rather use
than their bare hands.
1.3.172-173.

I do perceive here a divided duty.
To you I am bound for life and education.
My life and education both do learn me
How to respect you. You are the lord of duty.
I am hitherto your daughter. But here's my husband.
And so much duty as my mother showed
To you, preferring you before her father,
So much I challenge that I may profess

Due to the Moor my lord.
1.3.180-188.

When remedies are past, the griefs are ended
by seeing the worst, which late on hopes depended.
1.3.202-203.

The robbed that smiles steals something from the thief;
He robs himself that spends a bootless grief.
1.3.207-208.

We must obey the time.
1.3.300.

It is silliness to live when to live is torment; and then have we a prescription to die when death is our physician.
1.3.308-309.

'Tis in ourselves that we are thus or thus.
Our bodies are our gardens to the which our wills are gardeners; so that if we will plant nettles or sow lettuce, set hyssop and weed up thyme, supply it with on gender of herbs or distract it with many, either to have it sterile with idleness or manur'd with industry- why the power and corrigible authority of this lies in our wills.
1.3.318-324.

I do beguile the thing I am by seeming otherwise.
2.1.122-123.

Fairness and wit;
The one's for the use and the other uses it.
2.1.130-131.

Base men being in love have then a nobility in their natures more than
is native to them
2.1.213-214.

If she had been blest than she would never have loved the Moor.
2.1.247-248.

For that I do suspect the lusty Moor
Hath leaped into my seat—the thought whereof
Doth, like a poisonous mineral, gnaw my inwards,
And nothing can or shall content my soul
Till I am evened with him, wife for wife,
Or, failing so, yet that I put the Moor
At least into a jealousy so strong
That judgment cannot cure.
2.1.289-296.

Knavery's plain face is never seen till us'd.
2.1.306.

Indeed, she is a most fresh and delicate creature.
2.3.20.

She is indeed perfection.
2.3.25.

England, where indeed they are most potent in potting.
2.3.80.

He is a soldier fit to stand by Caesar
And give direction.
2.3.115-116.

Reputation is an idle and most false imposition; oft got without merit, and lost without deserving.
2.3.260-261.

When devils will their blackest sins put on, they do suggest at first with heavenly shows, as I do now.
2.3.340-342.

How poor are they that have not patience!
2.3.358.

Dull not device by coldness and delay.
2.3.376.

The heavens forbid but that our loves and comforts should

increase even as our days do grow.
3.1.192-194.

If I do vow a friendship I'll perform it
to the last article.
3.3.20-21

If thou dost love me, show me thy thought.
3.3.119-120.

Men should be that they seem; or those that be not, would they might seem none!
3.3.131-132.

He that filches from me my good name robs me of that which not enriches him and makes me poor indeed.
3.3.163-165.

I'll see before I doubt; when I doubt, prove;
3.3.194.

O curse of marriage,
that we can call these delicate creatures ours,
and not their appetites!
3.3.272-273.

If she be false, o, then heaven mocks itself!
3.3.282.

It is a common thing... to have a foolish wife.
3.3.307- 309.

I swear 'tis better to be much abus'd
Than but to know't a little.
3.3.339-340.

He that is robb'd, not wanting what is stol'n,
Let him not know't, and he's not robb'd at all.
3.3.346-347.

I should be wise; for honesty's a fool,
And loses that it works for.

3.3.385-386.

Sure there's some wonder in this handkerchief;
I'm most unhappy at the loss of it.
3.4.101.

'Tis not a year or two shows us a man.
they are all but stomachs, and we all but food;
They eat us hungerly, and when they are full,
They belch us.
3.4.104-107.

Lovers absent hours, more tedious than the dial eight score times.
O weary reckoning!
3.4.175-177.

I never knew a woman love man so.
4.1.110.

They laugh that win.
4.1.122.

O, she will sing the savageness out of a bear!
4.1.185-186.

If that the earth could teem with woman's tears,
Each drop she falls would prove a crocodile.
4.1.241-242.

Would thou had'st never been born!
4.2.70.
O balmy breath, that dost almost persuade
Justice to break her sword! One
more, one more.
Be thus when thou art dead, and I will kill thee
And love thee after. One more, and this the last.
5.2.16-20.

Nobody. I. Myself. Fairwell.
5.2.126.

O who hath done this deed?
Thou art as rash as fire to say
That she was false. Oh she was heavenly true!
5.2.138-139.

O thou Othello, that was once so good,
Fall'n in the practice of a damned slave,
What shall be said to thee?
5.2.294-296.

Then must you speak
Of one not easily jealous, but, being wrought,
Perplexed in the extreme; of one whose hand,
Like the base Indian, threw a pearl away
Richer than all his tribe; of one whose subu'd eyes,
Albeit unused to the melting mood,
Drop tears as fast as the Arabian trees
Their med'cinable gum. Set you down this;
And say besides that in Aleppo once,
Where a malignant and a turban'd Turk
Beat a Venetian and traduc'd the state,
I took by th' throat the circumsis'd dog,
and smote him- thus.
5.2.346-358.

JULIUS CAESAR

Beware the ides of march.
1.2.17.

If I have veil'd my look,
I turn the trouble of my countenance
Merely upon myself.
1.2.37-39.

The eye sees not itself but by reflection, by some other things.
1.2.53-54.

I love
the name of honour more than I fear death.
1.2.88-89.

I had as lief no be as live to be in awe of such a thing as I myself.
I was born as free as Caesar; so were you.
1.2.95-97.

Men at some time are masters of their fates;
the fault, dear Brutus, is not in our stars,
but in ourselves
1.2.139-141.
It is the part of men to fear and tremble
When the most mighty gods by tokens
Send such dreadful heralds to astonish us.
1.3.54-56.

Cassius from bondage will deliver Cassius.
1.3.90.

That part of tyranny that I do bear,
I can shake off at pleasure.
1.3.98-99.

What trash is Rome,
w rubbish, and what offal, when it serves
for the base matter to illuminate
so vile a thing as Caesar!
1.3.108-111.

For my part, I know no personal cause to spurn at him.
2.1.10-11.

O conspiracy,
Sham'st thou to show thy dang'rous brow by night,
When evils are most free? O, then, by day
Where wilt thou find a cavern dark enough
To mask thy monstrous visage? Seek none,
conspiracy.
Hide it in smiles and affability;
For if thou path, thy native semblance on,
Not Erebus itself were dim enough
To hide thee from prevention.
2.1.77-85.

Let's be sacrifice, but not butchers, Caius.
2.1.166.

What need we but our own cause to prick us to redress?
2.1.123-124.

Let's be sacrificers, but not butchers, Cauis.
We all stand up against the spirit of Caesar,
and in the spirit of men there is no blood.
O that we then could come by Caesar's spirit,
and not dismember Caesar! But alas,
Caesar must bleed for it!
2.1.166-171.

Let not our looks put on our purposes.
2.1.225.

Now bid me run,
and I will strive with things impossible;

yea, get the better of them.
2.1.324-326.

Cowards die many times before their deaths
2.2.32.

Danger knows full well that caesar is more dangerous than he.
2.2.44-45.

Your wisdom is consum'd in confidence.
2.2.48.

Have I in conquest stretch'd mine arm so far,
to be afeard to tell greybeards the truth?
2.2.66-67.

Security gives way to conspiracy.
2.3.5.

How hard it is for women to keep counsel!
2.4.9.

How weak a thing the heart of a woman is!
2.4.38-39.

I am constant as the Northern Star,
of whose true-fix'd and resting quality
there is no fellow in the firmament.
3.1.60-62.

Et tu, Brute? Then fall caesar!
3.1.77.

Liberty! Freedom! Tyranny is dead!
3.1.78.

How many ages hence
Shall this our lofty scene be acted over
In states unborn and accents yet unknown!
3.1.112-114.

Live a thousand years, I shall not find myself so apt to die.
3.1.160-161.

Your voice shall be as strong as any man's
In the disposing of new dignities.
3.1.178-179.
Pardon me, Julius! Here wast thou bayed, brave
hart, here didst thou fall, and here thy hunters stand
Signed in thy spoil and crimsoned in thy Lethe.
O world, thou wast the forest to this hart,
And this indeed, O world, the heart of thee.
How like a deer strucken by many princes
Dost thou here lie!
3.1.205-211.

This foul deed shall smell above the earth
3.1.275.

Friends, Romans, Countrymen, lend me your ears
I come to bury Caesar, not to praise him.
3.2. 73-74.

This was the most unkindest of all;
For when the noble Caesar saw him stab,
Ingratitude, more strong than traitors' arms,
Quite vanquishe'd him. Then burst his mighty heart (.)
3.2.182-186.

Here was a caesar! When comes such another?
3.2.253.

When love begins to sicken and decay,
it useth an enforced ceremony.
4.1.20-21.

Did not great Julius bleeed for justice sake?
What villain touch'd his body, that did stab,
and not for justice?
4.3.19-21.

I am arm'd so strong in honesty
that they pass by me as the idle wind,
which I respect not.
4.3.67-69.

Good reasons, must, of force, give place to better.
4.3.201.

On such a full sea are we not afloat,
And we must take the current when it serves,
Or lose our ventures.
4.3.220-222.

Think not, thou noble Roman,
That ever Brutus will go bound to Rome.
He bears too great a mind. But this same day
Must end that work the ides of March begun.
And whether we shall meet again, I know not.
5.1.110-114.

O that a man might know
the end of this day's business ere it come!
5.2.122-123.

Come now, keep thine oath;
Now be a freeman, and with this good sword,
Than ran through Caesar's bowels, search this bosom.
Stand not to the answer; here, take thou the hilts;
And when my face is cover'd, as 'tis now,
Guide thou the sword.
5.3.40-44.

Are yet two Romans living such as these?
The last of all the Romans, fare thee well!
5.3.98-99.

Keep this man safe;
Give him all kindness. I had rather have
Such men my friends than enemies.
5.4.27-30.

His life was gentle; and the elements
so mix'd in him that Nature might stand up
and say to all the world 'This was a man!'
5.5.75.

WILLIAMSHAKESPEARE

ROMEO AND JULIET

Could we but learn from whence his sorrows grow, we would as willingly give cure as we know.
1.1.152-153

Sad hours seem long.
1.1.161

He that is stricken blind cannot forget
the precious treasure of his eyesight lost.
1.1.230-231

Younger than she are happy mothers made.
1.2.12.

Tut, man, one fire burns out another burning.
one pain is less'ned by another anguish.
1.2.45-46

Take thou some new infection to thy eye,
and the rank poison of the old will die.
1.2.49-50

Dost though fall upon thy face? Thou will fall backward when thou hast more wit.
1.3.41-42

Go girl, seek happy nights to happy days.
1.3.105

You have dancing shoes with nimble soles; I have a soul of lead.
1.4.14-15

Is love a tender thing? It is too rough,
too rude, too boist'rous , and it pricks like thorn.
1.4.25-26

If love be rough with you, be rough with love.

1.4.27

I talk of dreams;
which are the idle children of an idle brain,
begot of nothing but vain fantasy
1.5.96-98

O, she doth teach the torches to burn bright!
1.5.43

Did my heart love till now? Forswear it, sight!
1.5.52

My lips, two blushing pilgrims, ready stand
To smooth that rough touch with a tender kiss.
Good pilgrim, you do wrong your hand too much,
Which mannerly devotion shows in this;
For saints have hands that pilgrims' hands do touch,
And palm to palm is holy palmers' kiss.
Have not saints lips, and holy palmers too?
Ay, pilgrim, lips that they must use in prayer.
O, then, dear saint, let lips do what hands do;
They pray, grant thou, lest faith turn to despair.
Saints do not move, though grant for prayers' sake.
Then move not, while my prayer's effect I take.
Thus from my lips, by yours, my sin is purged.
Then have my lips the sin that they have took.
1.5.93-106

My only love sprung from my only hate!
1.5.139

Can I go forward when my heart is here?
2.1.1.

If love be blind, love cannot hit the mark.
2.1.33.

He jests at scars that never felt a wound.
2.2.1

But soft! What light through yonder window breaks?

It is the east, and Juliet is the sun.
Arise, fair sun, and kill the envious moon,
Who is already sick and pale with grief,
That thou, her maid, art far more fair than she.
Be not her maid since she is envious.
Her vestal livery is but sick and green,
And none but fools do wear it. Cast it off!
It is my lady. Oh, it is my love.
Oh, that she knew she were!
She speaks, yet she says nothing. What of that?
Her eye discourses. I will answer it.
I am too bold. Tis not to me she speaks.
Two of the fairest stars in all the heaven,
Having some business, do entreat her eyes
To twinkle in their spheres till they return.
What if her eyes were there, they in her head?
The brightness of her cheek would shame those stars
As daylight doth a lamp. Her eye in heaven
Would through the airy region stream so bright
That birds would sing and think it were not night.
See how she leans her cheek upon her hand.
Oh, that I were a glove upon that hand
That I might touch that cheek!
2.2.2-25.

What's in a name? That which we call a rose by any other name would smell as sweet. So Romeo would, were he not Romeo called, retain that dear perfection which he owes without that title. Romeo, doff thy name.
2.2.43-46.

Do not swear at all;
or if thou wilt, swear by they gracious self,
which is the god of my idolatry,
and I'll believe thee.
2.2.112-114.

This bud of love, by summer's ripening breath,
may prove a beauteous flow'r when next we meet.
2.2.121-123.

Love goes toward love as schoolboys from their books;
But love from love, toward school with heavy looks.
2.2.157-158.

Good night, good night! Parting is such sweet sorrow,
that I shall say good night till it be tomorrow.
2.185-186.

Virtue turns itself to vice, being misapplied.
2.3.21.

Holy Saint Francis!
2.3.65.

Young men's love then lies
not truly in their hearts, but in their eyes.
2.3.68-69.

Women may fall when there's no strength left in men.
2.3.80.

Wisely and slow; they stumble that run fast.
2.3.94.

A gentleman, nurse, that loves to hear himself talk
and will speak more in a minute than he will stand to in a month.
2.4.139-140.

But come what sorrow can,
it cannot countervail the exchange of joy
that one short minute gives me in her sight.
2.6.3-6.

These violent delights have violent ends
And in their triumph die, like fire and powder,
Which, as they kiss, consume. The sweetest honey is loathsome
in his own deliciousness
And in the taste confounds the appetite.
Therefore, love moderately; long love doth so.
Too swift arrives as tardy as too slow.
2.6.9-15.

For now, these hot days the mad blood is stirring.
3.1.4.

I will not budge for no mans pleasure, I.
3.1.54.

The love I bear thee can afford no better terms than this; thou are at villain.
3.1.59-60.

No, 'tis not so deep as a well, nor so wide as a church door; but tis enough, 'twill serve. As for me tomorrow, and you shall find me a grave man.
3.1.93-97.

O, I am fortune's fool!
3.1.134.

If love be blind, it best agrees with night.
3.2.9-10.

Was ever book containing such vile matter so fairly bound?
3.2.83-84.

There's no trust, no faith, no honesty in men
3.2.85-86.

Thou canst not speak of that thou dost not feel.
3.3.64.

Thy wit, that ornament to shape and love,
Misshapen in the conduct of them both,
Like powder in a skill-less soldier's flask
Is set afire. by thine own ignorance.
3.3.130-134.

O, what learning is!
3.3.160.

All these woes shall seve for sweet discourses in our times to come.
3.5.52.

Is there no pity in the clouds that sees into the bottom of my grief?
3.5.198-199.

Love give me strength!
4.1.125.

My heart is wondrous light,
Since this same wayward girl is so reclaimed.
4.2.46-47.

My dismal scene I needs must act alone.
4.3.19.

Death lies upon her like an untimely frost
Upon the sweetest flower of all the field.
4.5.28-29.

Never was seen so black a day as this.
4.5.54.

For though fond nature bids us all lament,
Yet nature's tears are reason's merriment.
4.5.81-82.

If I may trust the flattering truth of sleep,
My dreams presage some joyful news at hand.
5.1.1-2.

O mischief, thou art swift
To enter in the thoughts of desperate men!
5.1.35-36.

The world is not thy friend, nor the world's law;
the world affords no law to make thee rich;
then be not poor, but break it and take this.
5.1.72-74.

His looks I fear, and his intents I doubt.
5.3.44.

How oft when men are at the point of death have they been merry!

5.1.88-89.

See what a scourge is laid upon your hate,
that heaven finds means to kill your joys with love.
5.2.292-293.

Never was a story of more woe,
than this of Juliet and her Romeo.
5.2.309-310.

TIMON OF ATHENS

Our poesy is as a gum, which oozes
From whence 'tis nourish'd.
1.1.23-24.

His means most short, his creditors most strait.
1.1.99.

I am not of that feather to shake off
My friend when he must need me.
1.1.103-104.

Know things of like value, differing in the owners, are prized by their masters.
1.1.172-174.

You mend the jewel by the wearing it.
1.1.175.

He that loves to be flattered is worthy o' the flatterer.
1.1.228.

Ceremony was but devis'd at first to set a gloss on faint deeds, hollow welcomes
1.2.15-16.

I wonder men dare trust themselves with men.
1.2.42.

I wonder men dare trust themselves with men.
Methinks they should invite them without knives.
Good for their meat, and safer for their lives.
There's much example for 't. The fellow that sits

next him, now parts bread with him, pledges the
breath of him in a divided draft, is the readiest
man to kill him. 'T 'as been proved. If I were a huge
man, I should fear to drink at meals,
Lest they should spy my wind-pipe's dangerous notes.
Great men should drink with harness on their throats.
1.2.42-52.

You had rather be at a breakfast of enemies than a dinner of friends.
1.2.73.

What need we have any friends if we should ne'er have need of em?
1.2.90.

We are born to do benefits, and what better or properer can we call our own than the riches of our friends?
1.2.98-99.

We make ourselves fools to disport ourselves,
And spend our flatteries to drink those men
Upon whose age we void it up again
With poisonous spite and envy.
1.2.130-133.

Happier is he that has no friend to feed
than such that do e'en enemies exceed.
1.2.200-201.

Honest fools lay out their wealth on curtsies
1.2.237.

O love and honour him,
but must not break my back to heal his finger.
2.1.23-24.

 A plague upon him, dog!
2.2.48.

There will little learning die, then, that day you art hang'd.

2.2.85.

And nature, as it grows again toward earth,
is fashion'd for the journey dull and heavy.
2.218-219.

Every man has his fault, and honesty is his.
3.1.28.

The devil knew not what he did when he made
man politic. He crossed himself by 't, and I cannot
think but, in the end, the villainies of man will set
him clear.
3.3.26-28.

Who cannot keep his health must keep his house.
3.3.41.

He's poor, and that's revenge enough.
3.4.63.

Pity is the virtue of the law.
3.5.8.

To revenge is no valour, but to bear.
3.5.39.

Why do fond men expose themselves to battle,
And not endure all threats?
3.5.42-43.

Why then, women are more vallaint,
That stay at home, if bearing carry it;
And the ass more captain than the lion the fellow
Loaden with irons wiser than the judge,
If wisdom be in suffering.
3.5.46-51.

Lend to each man enough, that one need
not lend to another; for, were your godheads to
borrow of men, men would forsake the gods. Make

the meat be beloved more than the man that gives it.
3.7.76-77.

For bounty, that makes gods, doest still mar men.
4.2.42.

We are fellows still,
serving alike in sorrow.
4.2.18-19.

Who would not wish to be from wealth exempt,
since riches point to misery and contempt?
4.2.31-32.

The learned pate
ducks to the golden fool.
4.3.17-18.

There's nothing level in our cursèd natures
But direct villainy
4.3.20-21.

Tell this whore of thine
hath in her more destruction than thy sword.
4.3.60-61.

Thy lips rot off!
4.3.62.

They love thee not that use thee.
4.3.83.

Willing misery outlives uncertain pomp.
4.3.252-243.

If thou hadst not been born the worst of men,
thou hadst been a knave and a flatterer.
4.3.273-274.

What beast couldst thou be
that were not subject to a beast? And what a beast

art thou already that seest not thy loss in
transformation!
4.3.340-342.

Would thou were clean enough to spit upon!
4.3.356.

I am sick of this false world, and will love nought
but even the mere necessities upon't.
4.3.373-374.

I am rapt and cannot cover
The monstrous bulk of this ingratitude
With any size of words.
5.1.61-64.

I thank them; and would send them back the plague
Could I but catch it for them.
5.1.135-136.

And by the hazard of the spotted die
Let die the spotted.
5.4.33-34.

Were not all unkind, nor all deserve
the common stroke of war.
5.4.21-22.

Here lies a wretched corpse, of wretched soul bereft.
5.4.70.

CYMBELINE

How fine this tyrant
Can tickle where she wounds!
1.1.84-85.1.

Thou'rt poison to my blood!
1.1.128.

There cannot be a pinch of death
More sharp than this.
1.130-131.

Her beauty and her brain go not together.
1.2.28.

She shines upon fools, lest the reflection should hurt her.
1.2.31.

Strange fowl light upon neighbouring ponds.
1.3.84.

It came in too suddenly; let it die as it was born.
1.3.115-116.

Can we not partition make with spectacles so precious
'twixt fair and foul?
1.6.35-38.

Satiate yet unsatisfied desire... ravening first the lamb,
longs after for the garbage.
1.6.47-48.

It is a recreation to be by and hear him mock the Frenchman.
1.6.72-73.

Since doubting things go ill often hurts more
than to be sure they do; for certainties

either are past remedies, or, timely knowing,
the remedy then born
1.6.94-97.

When a gentleman is dispos'd to swear, it is not for any standers-by to curtail his oath.
2.1.10-11.

I am not vex'd more at anything in th' earth.
2.1.14.

He's a strange fellow, and knows not himself.
2.1.33.

Man's o'er-laboured sense repairs itself by rest.
2.2.10-11.

O sleep, thou ape of death.
2.2.31.

Here's a voucher stronger than ever law could make.
2.2.39-40.

Their deer to th' stand o' th' stealer; and tis gold
which makes the true man kill'd and saves the thief.
2.2.69-71.

There be no honour where there is no beauty.
2.6.109-110.

We will nothing pay for wearing our own noses.
3.1.13-14.

If it be so to do good service, never
let me be counted serviceable.
3.2.13-14.

Lovers and men in dangerous bonds pray not alike;
though forfeiters you cast in prison, yet you clasp young Cupids tables.
3.2.35-38.

The gates of monarchs are arch'd so high that giants may get thorough and keep their impious turbans on without good

morrow to the sun.
3.3.4-7.

Haply this life is best, if quite life be best.
3.3.29-30.

How hard it is to hide the sparks of nature!
3.3.79.

Their thoughts do hit
the roofs of palaces, and nature prompts them
in simple and low things to prince it much
beyond the trick of others.
3.3.83-86.

Slander, whose edge is sharper than the sword.
3.4.31-32.

Men's vows are women's traitors.
3.4.51-52.

Those that are betray'd do feel the treason sharply,
yet the traitor stands in worse case of woe.
3.4.83-85.

If I were as wise as honest,
then my purpose would prove well.
3.4.117-118.

I love and hate her; for she's fair and royal,
and that she hath all courtly parts more exquisite
than lady, ladies, woman.
3.5.71-73.

I'll be merry in my revenge.
3.5.145-146.

Man's life is a tedious one.
3.6.1.

Will poor folks lie, that have afflictions on them, knowing tis
a punishment or trial?
Yes; no wonder, when rich ones scarce tell true.

3.6.9-12.

Falsehood is worse in kings than beggars.
3.6.13-14.

The seat of industry would dry and die
but for the end it works to.
3.6.31-32.

Weariness can snore upon the flint, when resty sloth
finds the down pillow hard.
3.6.33-35.

Clay and clay differs in dignity,
whose dust is both alike.
4.2.4-5.

The breach of custom is breach of all.
4.2.10-11.

Society is no comfort to one not sociable.
4.2.12-13.

Cowards father cowards and base things base.
4.2.26.

Experience, O, thou disprov'st report!
4.2.34.

Those that I reverence, those I fear-- the wise;
at fools I laugh, not fear them.
4.2.96-97.

Defect of judgment is oft the cease of fear.
4.2.112-113.

Not Hercules could have knock'd out his brains, for he had none
4.2.115-116.

All solemn things should answer solemn accidents.
4.2.192-193.

For notes of sorrow out of tune are worse than priests and fanes
that lie.

4.2.242-243.

Our very eyes are sometimes, like our judgments, blind.
4.2.302-303.

Some falls are means the happier to arise.
4.2.406.

Every good servant does not all commands.
5.1.6.

Nothing routs us but the villainy of our fears.
5.2.12-13.

Who dares not stand his foe I'll be his friend.
5.3.60.

How man would have given their honours
to have sav'd their carcasses.
5.3.66-67.

Many dreams not to find, neither deserve,
and yet are steep'd in favours.
5.4.131-132.

He that sleeps feels not the toothache.
5.4.170.

I never saw such noble fury in so poor a thing.
5.5.7-8.

Who is't can read a woman?
5.5.47.

The temple of virtue was she.
5.5.220.

TROILUS AND CRESSIDA

I am weaker than a woman's tear .
1.1.8.

He that will have a cake out of the wheat must needs tarry the grinding.
1.1.15-16.

Nay, you must stay
the cooling too, or you may chance burn your lips.
1.1.25-26.

Sorrow that is couch'd in seeming gladness
Is like that mirth fate turns to sudden sadness.
1.1.39-40.

I speak no more than truth
thou dost not speak so much.
1.1.63-64.

Do you know a man if you see him?
1.2.61.

Is not birth, beauty, good shape, discourse, manhood, learning, gentleness, virtue, youth, liberality and such-like the spice and salt that season a man?
1.2.224-246.

In the reproof of chance lies the true proof of men.
1.3.33-34.

What honey is expected? Degree being vizarded,
The unworthiest shows as fairly in the mask.
1.3.83-84.

When the planets in evil mixture to disorder wander,

what plagues and what portents, what mutiny,
what raging of the sea, shaking of the earth,
commotion in the winds!
1.3.94-98.

O, when degree is shak'd,
which is the ladder of all high designs,
the enterprise is sick!
1.3.101-103.

Appetite, a universal wolf,
so doubly seconded with will and power,
must make perforce a universal prey,
and last eat up himself.
1.3.121-124.

The nature of the sickness found, Ulysses,
What is the remedy?
1.3.140-141.

They tax our policy and call it cowardice,
Count wisdom as no member of the war,
Forestall presci3nce and esteem no act
But that of hand.
1.3.198-201.

The worthiness of praise disdains his worth,
if that the prais'd himself bring the praise forth.
1.3.241-242.

Though it be sportful combat,
Yet in this trial much opinion dwells.
1.3.335-336.

A man distill'd out of our virtues.
1.3.350-351.

I will beat thee into handsomeness.
2.1.13-14.

You whoreson cur!
2.1.39.

Thou stool for a witch!
2.1.41.

You scurvy villain ass!
2.1.44.

I thou use to beat me, I will begin at thy heel and tell what thou art by inches, thou thing of no bowels, thou.
2.1.246-247.

Modest doubt is call'd
The beacon of the wise.
2.2.15-16.

'Tis mad idolatry to make the service greater than the god.
2.2.56-57.

She is not worth what she doth cost the keeping.
2.2.60.

Why, she is a pearl whose price hath launch'd above a thousand ships, and turn'd crown'd kings to merchants.
2.2.81-83.

O theft most base,
That we have stol'n what we do fear to keep!
2.2.92-93.

Nature craves all dues be rend'red to their owners.
2.2.173-174.

To their benumbèd wills, resist the same,
There is a law in each well-ordered nation
To curb those raging appetites that are
Most disobedient and refractory.
2.2.178-181.

The common curse of mankind, folly and ignorance be thine in great revenue!
2.3.24-25.

The amity that wisdom knits not, folly may easily untie.
2.3.98.

A stirring dwarf we do allowance give before a sleeping giant.
2.3.133-134.

Whatever praises itself but in the deed devours the deed in the praise.
2.3.152-153.

I do hate a proud man as I do hate the engender'ing of toads.
2.3.154.

Sweet, above thought I love thee.
3.1.152.

What folly I commit, I dedicate to you.
3.2.100.

You are wise-- or else you love not; for to be wise and love exceeds man's might; that dwells with gods above.
3.2.151-153.

When right with right wars who shall be most right?
3.2.168.

Pride hath no other glass to show itself but pride.
3.3.47-48.

For men, like butterflies,
Show not their mealy wings but to the summer.
3.3.78-79.

The beauty that is borne here in the face
the bearer knows not but commends itself
to others' eyes.
3.3.103-105.

While pride is fasting in his wantonness!
3.3.137.

Good deeds past, which are devour'd
as fast as they are made, forgot as soon
as done. Perseverance, dear my lord,
keeps honour bright.
3.3.148-151.

For honour travels in a strait so narrow
Where on but goes abreast.
3.3.153-154.

O, let not virtue seek
remuneration for the thing it was;
for beauty, wit, high birth, vigour of bone, desert in service, love,
friendship, charity, are subjects all
to envious and calumniating time.
3.3.169-174.

Things in motion sooner catch the eye
than what stirs not.
3.3.183-184.

The fool slides oe'r the ice that you should break.
3.3.215.

A woman impudent and mannish grown is not more loath'd than
an effeminate man in time of action.
3.3.217-218.

Wounds heal ill that men do give themselves.
3.3.229.

My love admits no qualifying dross;
No more my grief, in such a precious loss.
4.4.9-10.
The end crowns all;
And that old common arbitrator, Time,
Will one day end it.
4.5.224-225.

We must use expostulation kindly,
for it is parting from us.
4.4.59.

Sometimes we are devils to ourselves,
when we will tempt the frailty of our powers,
Presuming on their changeful potency.
4.4.94-96.

O sir, to such as boasting show their scars
A mock is due.
4.5.290-291.

With too much blood and too little brain these two may run mad;
but, if with too much brain and too little blood they do, I'll be a
curer of madmen.
5.1.46-48.

Welcome princes all.
5.1.68.

Tempt me no more to folly.
5.2.18.

How the devil luxury, with his fat rump and potato finger, tickles
these together!
5.2.55-56.

O beauty! Where is thy faith?
5.2.66.

One eye yet looks on thee;
but with my hear the other eye doth see.
5.2.105-106.

Shall I not lie in publishing truth?
5.2.118.

Never did young man fancy with so eternal and so fix'd a soul.
5.2.163-164.

It is the purpose that makes strong the vow;
but vows to every purpose must not hold.
5.3.23-24.

Words, words, mere words, no matter from the heart.
5.3.108.

Lechery eats itself.
5.4.32.

I am a bastard too. I love bastards. I am
bastard begot, bastard instructed, bastard in mind,
bastard in valor, in everything illegitimate. One
bear will not bite another, and wherefore should
one bastard? Take heed: the quarrel's most ominous
to us. If the son of a whore fight for a whore,
he tempts judgment. Farewell, bastard.
5.8.16-21.

TITUS ANDRONICUS

Be as just and gracious unto me as I am confident and kind to thee
1.1.61- 62.

Wilt thou draw near the nature of the gods?
Draw near them then in being merciful.
Sweet mercy is nobility's true badge.
1.1.117-119.

Let not discontent
Daunt your hopes.
1.1.167-268.

These words are razors to my wounded heart.
1.1.314.

Thy years wants wit, thy wits wants edge
2.1.26.

She is a woman, therefore may be woo'd;
she is a woman, therefore may be won.
2.1.82-83.

Ah my sweet Moor, sweeter to me than life!
2.3.51.

The worse to her the better lov'd of me.
2.3.167.

How easily murder is discovered!
2.3.287.

Sorrow concealed, like an oven stopp'd,

doth burn the heart to cinders where it is.
2.4.36-37.

O, could our mourning ease thy misery!
2.4.57.

Let us that have our tongues
plot some device of further misery
to make us donder'd at in time to come.
3.1.133-135.

If that be call'd deceit, I will be honest.
3.1.189.

Let fools do good, and fair men call for grace.
3.1.205.

If there were reasons for these miseries,
then into limits could I bind my woes.
3.1.220-221.

You heavy people, circle me about
That I may turn me to each one of you
 And swear unto my soul to right your wrongs.
3.1.276-278.

So, so, now sit; and look you eat no more
Than will preserve these bitter woes of ours.
3.2.1-2.

Alas, poor man! Grief has so wrought on him
He takes false shadows for true substances.
3.2.79-80.

Why should nature build so foul a den,
unless the gods delight in tragedies?
4.1.60-61.

O heavens, can you hear a good man groan
and not relent, or not compassion him?

4.1.124-125.

Pray to the devils; the gods have given us over.
4.2.46-47.

Why then she is the devil's dam.
4.2.64.

Is black so base a hue?
4.2.71.

Two may keep counsel when the third's away.
4.2.144.

We will solicit heaven and move the gods
to send down Justice for to wreak our wrongs.
4.3.49-50.

But where the bull and cow are both milk-white,
They never do beget a coal-black calf.
5.1.31-32.

This is the incarnate devil.
5.1.40.

For that I know
An idiot holds his bauble for a god,
And keeps the oath which by that god he swears,
To that I'll urge him.
5.1.78-81.

Tell him revenge is come to join with him,
and work confusion on his enemies
5.2.7-8.

Revenge, which makes the foul offender quake.
5.2.40.

We worldly men have miserable, mad, mistaking eyes.
5.2.66-67.

Long have I been forlorn, and all for thee.

5.2.81.

Welcome, dread Fury, to my woeful house,
Rapine and Murder, you are welcome too.
5.2.82-83.

Villains, for shame you could not beg for grace.
5.2.180.

I will grind your bones to dust,
and with your blood and it I'll make a paste;
and of the paste a coffin I will rear,
and make to two pastries of your shameful heads
5.2.186-190.

When no friends are by, men praise themselves.
5.3.118.

Ah, why should wrath be mute and fury dumb?
I am no baby, I, that with base prayers
I should repent the evils I have done;
Ten thousand worse than ever yet I did
Would I perform, if I might have my will.
If one good deet in all my life I did,
I do repent it from my very soul.
5.3.184-190.

THE HISTORIES

Some of Shakespeare's greatest work is in his histories. He recreates great moments by adding the spice of liberal interpretation and enhanced weight to historical characters. Under Shakespeare's pen, historical figures grow more human through the expression he gives them. Perhaps this is seen by none other than the fat, drunken, clever, and comely John Falstaff from Henry IV part 1- Henry V, as well as The Merry Wives of Windsor.

Falstaff, one of literature's greatest figures, the very personification of "Carpe Diem" and wisdom surpassing convention, is based off of a real person (or a few, depending on your interpretation of him). His real connection to Hal of Henry the IV (who becomes King Henry the V) is a bit unclear. But given how Shakespeare crafted him into an iconic character, it is hardly important. The place of Falstaff in our psyche and culture surpasses simple history.

Shakespeare's Falstaff lives in his plays, in our pop culture, and in our imaginations- the archetypical fat man living life without care beyond enjoyment and self-preservation. He bends rules we all know we would like to- rules about Honor, for example, that lead to an early death. We see the truth of a fool's life in Falstaff and this resonates. Falstaff, a historical figure largely forgotten otherwise achieves immortality via the permanent grandness Shakespeare breathes into him. Shakespeare's dream surpasses the historical fact while keeping faith with enough core truths to call his plays "Histories".

If that doesn't whet your appetite for Shakespeare's Histories, perhaps these amazing quotes will.

Order of the Histories:

King John
Richard the II
Henry the IV, Part 1
Henry the IV, Part 2
Henry the V
Henry the VI, Part 1
Henry the VI, Part 2
Henry the VI, Part 3
Richard the III
Henry the VIII

KING JOHN

Truth is truth.
1.1.104.

By chance, not by truth.
1.1.169.

Who dare not stir by day must walk by night;
And have is have, however men do catch.
1.1.171-172.

Sweet, Sweet, Sweet poison for the age's tooth.
1.1.213.

Madam, I would not wish a better father.
1.1.260.

He that perforce robs lions of their hearts
may easily win a woman's.
1.1.268.

The peace of heaven is their that lift their swords
In such a just and charitable war.
2.1.35-36.

That right in peace which here we urge in war,
and then we shall repent each drop of blood
that hot rash haste so indirectly shed.
2.1.46-48.

You are the hare of whom the proverb goes,
whose valour plucks dead lions by the beard.
2.1.137-138.

I would that I were low laid in my grave;
I am not worth this coil that's made for me.
2.1.164-165.

Thou monstrous slanderer of heaven and earth!
Thou monstrous injurer of heaven and earth
2.1.172-173.

I was never so bethum'p with words!
2.1.466.

I do protest I never lov'd myself
Till now I infixed I beheld myself
Drawn in the flattering table of her eye.
2.1.501-503.

Well, whiles I am a beggar, I will rail
and say there is no sin but to be rich;
and being rich, my virtue then shall be
to say there is no vice but beggary.
2.1.593-596.

I trust I may not trust thee, for thy word
is but the vain breath of a common man.
3.1.7-8.

Thou wear a lion's hide! Doft if for shame,
And hang a calf's skin on those recreant limbs.
3.1.127-128.

I may disjoin my hand, but not my faith.
3.1.262.

I will instruct my sorrows to be proud,
for grief is proud, and makes his owner stoop.
3.1.68-69.

My grief's so great, that no supporter but the huge firm earth can hold it up.
3.1.71-72.

When law can do no right,
let it be lawful that law bar no wrong.
3.1.185-186.

The sun is in the heaven, and the proud day,

attended with the pleasures of the world,
is all to wanton and too full of gawds
to give me audience.
3.3.32-36.

If that thou could'st see me without eyes,
hear me without thine ears, and make reply
without a tongue, using conceit alone,
without eyes, ears, and harmful sound of words--
then in despite of brooded watchful day,
I would into thy bosom pour my thoughts.
3.3.47-53.

All shall yet go well.
3.4.4.

What can go well when we have run so ill?
3.3.5.

There's nothing in this world can make me joy.
3.4.107.

Life is as tedious as a twice-told tale, vexing the dull ear of a drowsy man; and bitter shame hath spoil';d the sweet world's taste, that it yields nought but shame and bitterness.
3.4.108-110.

Strong reasons make strong actions.
3.4.182.

I should be as merry as the day is long.
4.1.18.

Feeling what small things are boisterous there,
your vile intent must needs seem horrible.
4.1.93-94.

There is no sure foundation set on blood,
No certain life achiev'd by others' death.
4.1.104-105.

To gild refined gold, to paint the lily,
to throw perfume on the violet,

to smooth the ice, or add another hue
unto the rainbow, or with taper-light
to seek the beauteous eye of heaven to garnish,
is wasteful and ridiculous excess.
4.2.11-16.

How oft the sights of means to do ill deeds
make deeds ill done
4.2.219.

Hostility and civil tumult reigns
between my conscience and my cousin's death.
4.2.247-248.

Heaven take my soul, and England keep my bones!
4.3.10.

Our griefs, and not our manners, reason now.
4.3.29.

The earth had not a hole to hide this deed.
4.3.36.

Trust not those cunning waters of his eyes,
For villainy is not without such rheum;
And he, long traded in it, make it seem like rivers of remorse and innocence.
4.3.107-110.

Be fire with fire
threaten the threat'ner, and outface the brow.
5.1.48-49.

And great affections wrestling in thy bosom
Doth make an earthquake of nobility.
5.2.41-42.

Thou art my friend that know'st my tongue so well.
5.6.8.

O, my sweet sir, news fitting to the night,
black, fearful, comfortless, and horrible.
5.6.19-20.

'Tis strange that death should sing.
5.7.20.

I am a scribbled form drawn with a pen
upon parchment, and against this fire
do I shrink up.
5.7.32-34.

RICHARD II

In rage, deaf as the sea, hasty as fire.
1.1.19.

Since the more fair and crystal is the sky,
The uglier seem the clouds that in it fly.
1.1.41-42.

God and good men hate so foul a liar.
1.1.114.

Mine honour is my life; both grow in one;
Take honour from me and my life is done.
1.1.182-183.

We were not born to sue, but to command.
1.1.196.

Grief boundeth where it falls.
1.2.68.

God in thy good cause make thee prosperous.
1.3.78.

I am too old to fawn upon a nurse,
too old in years to be a pupil now.
1.3.170-171.

Since thou hast far to go, bear not along
the clogging burden of a guilty soul.
1.3.199-200.

Things sweet to taste prove in digestion sour.
1.3.236.

Grief makes one hour ten.
1.3.261.

There is no virtue in necessity.
1.3.278.

The apprehension of the good
gives but the greater feeling to the worse.
1.3.300-301.

Where words are scarce they are seldom spent in vain.
2.1.7.

More are men's ends marked than their lives before.
2.1.11.

The task he undertakes
is numb'ring sands and drinking oceans dry.
2.2.146.

I count myself in nothing else so happy
as in a soul rememb'ring my good friends.
2.3.46-47.

Though death be poor, it ends a mortal woe.
3.1.152.

Not all the water in the rough rude sea
can wash the balm off from an anointed king.
3.2.55-56.

Weak men must fall; for heaven still guards the right.
3.2.61.

Cry woe, destruction, ruin and decay—
The worst is death and death will have his day.
3.2.102-103.

The breath of worldly men cannot depose
the deputy elected by the lord.
3.2.56-57.

All goes worse than I have power to tell.
3.2.120.

Sweet love, I see, changing his property,
turns the sourest and most deadly hate.
3.2.135-136.

And nothing can we call our own but death
And that small model of the barren earth
Which servs as paste and cover to our bones.
3.2.178-179.

He does me double wrong
that wounds me with the flatteries of his tongue.
3.2.215-216.

My legs can keep no measure in delight
When my poor heart no measure keeps in grief.
3.4.6-8.

Your cares set up do not pluck my cares down.
4.1.195.

Yet you pilates
Have here deliver'd me to my sour cross,
And water cannot wash away your sins.
4.1.240-242.

Hath sorrow struck so many blows upon this face of mine and made no deeper wounds?
4.1.277-279.

Yet look up, behold, that you in pity may dissolve to dew,
and wash him fresh again with true-love tears.
5.1.8-10.

The truth of what we are shows but this: I am sworn brother, sweet, to grim necessity; and he and I will keep a league till death.
5.1.19-21.

The lion dying thrusteth forth his paw,
and wounds the earth if nothing else, with rage,

to be o'erpow'r'd.
5.1.29-31.

The love of wicked men converts to fear.
5.1.66.

My guilt be on my head, and ther's an end.
5.1.69.

So two, together weeping, make one woe.
5.1.86.

The eyes of men, after a well-grac'd actor leaves the stage, are idly bent on him that enters next, thinking his prattle to be tedious.
5.2.23-26.

My heart is not confederate with my hand.
5.3.52.

Forget to pity him, lest thy pity prove
a serpent that will sing thee to the heart.
5.3.57-58.

Thy overflow of good converts to bad.
5.3.63.

Mine honour lives when his dishonour dies.
5.3.70.

Love loving not itself, none other can.
5.3.98.

His eyes do drop no tears, his prayers are in jest.
5.3.101.

I have been studying how I may compare
this prison where I live unto the world
and, for because the world is populous
and here is not a creature but myself,
I cannot do it. Yet I'll hammer it out.
5.5.1-5.

Thoughts tending to content flatter themselves
that they are not the first of fortunes slaves

nor shall not be the last; like silly beggars
who sitting in the stocks, refuge their shame.
5.5.23-26.

Thus play I in one person so many people
And none contented.
5.5.30-31.

Sometimes am I king;
then treasons make me wish myself a beggar,
and so I am. Then crushing penury
Persuades me I was better when a king;
then am I king'd again.
5.5.32-36.

How sour sweet music is
when time is broke and no proportion kept!
So it is in the music of men's lives.
5.5.42-44.

I was not made a horse;
And yet I bear a burden like an ass.
5.5.92-93.

What my tongue dares not, that my heart shall say.
5.5.97.

Patience is stale, and I am weary of it.
5.5.103.

Great king, within this coffin I present thy buried fear.
5.6.29-30.

They love not poison that do poison need.
5.6.38.

My soul is full of woe
that blood should sprinkle me to make me grow.
5.6.44-45.

THE GREAT BIG BOOK OF SHAKESPEARE QUOTES

HENRY IV PART 1

It is a conquest for a prince to boast of.
1.1.78.

What a devil hast thou to do with the time of day?
1.2.4-5.

I would to God thou and I knew where a commodity of good names were to bought.
1.2.80-81.

Wisdom cries out in the streets, and no man regards it.
1.2.86.

'Tis no sin for a man to labour in his vocation.
1.2.101.

O, if men were to be saved by merit, what hole in hell were hot enough for him?
1.2.104-105.

Give the devil his due.
1.2.114.

There's neither honesty, manhood, nor good fellowship in thee.
1.2.134.

If all the years were playing holidays,
To sport would be as tedious as to work;
But when they seldom come, they wish'd-for come.
1.2.197-199.

Respect, which the proud soul never pays but to the proud.
1.3.9.

O, the blood more stirs to rouse a lion than to start a hare!

1.3.196-197.

Why, what a wasp stung and impatient fool art thou to break into this woman's mood,
Tying thine ear to no tongue but thine own?
1.3.236-238.

Why, thou knowest I'm as valiant as Hercules.
1.4.235.

A plague upon you both!
2.1.16.

Were't not for laughing, I should pity him.
2.2.107.

Out of this nettle, danger, we pluck the flower, safety.
2.3.6-7.

Since you love me not,
I will not love myself.
2.3.94-95.

There is nothing but roguery to be found in villainous man.
2.4.117-118.

That's past praying for.
2.4.183.

Is not the truth the truth?
2.4.224.

Trickling tears are vain.
2.5.381.

The more it is trodden on the faster it grows.
2.4.387-388.

Yet youth, the more it is wasted the sooner it wears.
2.4.389.

Him keep with; the rest, banish.
2.4.417.

That old white-bearded satan.
2.4.446.

If sack and sugar be a fault, God help the wicked.
2.4.452.

I do, I will.
2.4.464.

Dost thou hear, Hal? Never call a true piece of gold counterfeit. Thou art essentially mad, without seeming so.
2.4.475.

Diseased nature oftentimes breaks forth in strange eruptions.
3.1.27-28.

I can teach thee, coz, to shame the devil by telling truth.
3.1.58-59.

O, he is as tedious as a tired horse, a railing wife; worse than a smokey house.
3.1.159-161.

By being seldom seen, I could not stir, but, like a comet, I was wond'red at.
3.2.46-47.

Whereof a little more than a little is by much too much.
3.2.72-73.

The end of life cancels all bands.
3.2.157.

Company, a villainous company, hath been the end of me.
3.3.9-10.

Do thou amend thy face and I'll amend my life.
3.3.25.

Why thou whoreson, impudent, emobss'd rascal.
3.3.155-156.

Wanton as youthful goats, wild as young bulls.
4.1.103.

I did never see such pitiful rascals.
4.2.62.

To the latter end of a fray and the beginning of a feast fits a dull fighter and keen guest.
4.2.77-78.

Nothing can seem foul to those that win.
5.1.8.

We stand opposed by such means as you yourself have forg'd against yourself
5.1.67-68.

Thou owest god a death.
5.1.126.

Honour pricks me on.
5.1.127-140.

Well, 'tis no matter; honour pricks me on. Yea, but how if honour prick me off when I come on? How then? Can honour set-to a leg? No. Or an arm? No. Or take away the grief of a wound? No. Honour hath no skill in surgery, then? No. What is honour? A word. What is in that word honour? What is that honour? Air. A trim reckoning! Who hath it? He that died 'o Wednesday. Doth he feel it? No. Doth he hear it? No. 'Tis insensible then? Yeah, to the dead. But will it no live with the living? No. Why? Detraction will not suffer it. Therefore I'll none of it. Honour is a mere scutcheon. And so ends my catechism.
5.1.129-139.

The time of life is short; to spend that shortness basely were too long.
5.2.82-83.

If we live, we live to tread on kings.
5.2.86.

Heaven to earth, some of us never shall a second time do such a courtesy.
5.2.100-101.

Who never promiseth but means to pay.
5.4.44.

Two stars keep not their motion in one sphere
5.4.66.

I better brook the loss of brittle life
than those proud titles thou hast won of me;
they wound my thoughts worse than thy sword my flesh;
But thoughts, the slaves of life, and life, time's fool,
and time, that takes survey of all the world,
must have a stop.
5.4.77-83.

Ill weaved ambition, how much art thou shrunk.
5.4.88.

This earth that bears thee dead
bears not alive so stout a gentleman.
5.4.92-93.

Could not all this flesh keep in a little life?
5.4.102-103.

I should have much miss of thee
If I were much in love with vanity.
5.4.104-105.

The better part of valour is discretion.
5.4.119.

Lord, Lord, how this world is given to lying!
5.4.143.

THE GREAT BIG BOOK OF SHAKESPEARE QUOTES

HENRY THE IV PART 2

Which of you will stop the vent of hearing when loud rumour speaks?
1.1.1-2.

The time are wild; contention, like a horse full of high feeding, madly hath broke loose
And bears down all before him.
1.1.8-10.

Contention, like a horse full of high feeding, madly hath broke loose and bears down all before him.
1.1.9-11.

 O, such a day,
So fought, so followed, and so fairly won,
Came not till now to dignify the times
Since Caesar's fortune.
1.1.20-23.

See what a ready tongue suspicion hath!
1.1.83.

He that but fears the thing he would not know
hath by instinct knowledge from other's eyes
1.1.85-86.

Your spirit is too true, your fears too certain.
1.1.92.

Yet the first bringer of unwelcome news
Hath but a losing office, and his tongue
Sounds ever after as a sullen bell,
Rememb'red tolling a departing friend.

1.1.110-103.

Divorce not wisdom from your honour.
1.1.162.

Men of all sorts take a pride to gird at me.
1.2.5.

I am not only witty in myself, but the cause that wit is in other men.
1.2.9-10.

It is worse shame to beg than to be on the worst side.
1.2.70.

I am as poor as Job, my lord, but no so patient.
1.2.119.

I would my means were greater and my waist slenderer.
1.2.134.

You that are old consider not the capacities of us that are young.
1.2.164-165.

I were better to be eaten to death with a rust than to be scoured to nothing with perpetual motion.
1.2.207-208.

A man can no more separate age and covetousness than 'a can part young limbs and lechery, but the gout galls the one, and the pox pinches the other; and so both the degrees prevent my curses.
1.2.217-219.

I can get no remedy against this consumption of the purse.
1.2.223.

A good wit will make use of anything. I will turn diseases to commodity.
1.2.231-232.

Past and to come seem best; things present, worst.
1.3.107.

I am well acquainted with your manner of wrenching the true cause the false way.
2.1.105-106.

How ill it follows, after you have laboured so hard, you should talk so idly!
2.2.27-28.

Come, you virtuous ass, you bashful fool.
2.2.72.

Wisdom be your guide.
2.3.6.

He was the mark and glass, copy and book that fashion'd others.
2.3.31-32.

You two never meet but you fall to some discord.
2.3.52-53.

You filthy bung, away!
2.3.120.

What! You poor, base, rascally, cheating, lack-linen mate!
2.3.115-116.

A rascal, bragging slave!
2.3.215.

Why, thou globe of sinful continents, what a life dost thou lead!
2.3.275.

His face is lucifer's privy kitchen where he did nothing but roast malt-worms.
2.3.320-321.

You see, my good wenches, how men of merit are sought after.

2.3.362-363.

A pox damn you, you muddy rascal!
2.4.39-40.

Hang yourself, you muddy conger, hang yourself.
2.4.51-52.

Is it not strange that desire should so many years outlive performance?
2.4.250.

Uneasy lies the head that wears a crown.
3.1.31.

O God! That one might read the book of fate,
And see the revolution of the times.
3.1.45-46.

Jesu, Jesu, the mad days that I have spent! And to see how many of my old acquaintances are dead!
3.2.32-33.

Death, as the psalmist saith, is certain to all; all shall die.
3.2.35.

So the son of the female is the shadow of the male.
3.2.129.

Lord, Lord, how subject we old men are to this vice of lying.
3.2.294-295.

We are all diseased.
4.1.54.

But he hath forc'd us to compel this offer;
And it proceeds from policy, not love.
4.1.146-147.

Against ill chances men are ever merry;
But heaviness foreruns the good event.

4.2.81-82.

He hath a tear for pity and a hand
open as day for melting charity.
4.4.31-32.

Will fortune never come with both hands full,
but write her fair words still in foulest letters?
4.4.103-104.

How quickly nature falls into revolt
when gold becomes her object!
4.5.66-67.

Thy wish was father ... to that thought.
4.5.93.

Commit the oldest sins in the newest kinds of ways
4.5.126-127.

Thou best of gold art worst of gold.
4.5.162.

A friend in the court is better than a penny in purse.
5.1.30-31.

Let me but bear your love, I'll bear your cares.
5.1.58.

O, it is much that a lie with a slight oath and a jest with a
sad brow will do with a fellow that never had the
ache in his shoulders.
5.1.80-81.

I am fortune's steward.
5.1.129.

I... do arm myself to welcome the condition of the time.
5.2.9-10.

Do nothing but eat and make good cheer,
and praise god for the merry year;

When flesh is cheap and females dear,
and lusty lads roam here and there,
so Merrily, and ever among so merrily.
5.3.17-21.

Women are shrews, both short and tall.
5.3.32.

Falstaff: What, is the old king dead?
Pistol: As nail in door.
5.3.119-120.

Blessed are they that have been my friends
5.3.136.

How ill white hairs become a fool and a jester!
5.5.48.

I have long dreamt of such a kind of man,
so surfeit-swelled, so old, and so profane;
But being awaked, I do despise my dream.
5.5.50-52.

Know the grave doth gape for three thrice wider than for other men
5.5.54-55.

HENRY THE V

Never came reformation in a flood.
1.1.34.

The strawberry grows underneath the nettle,
And wholesome berries thrive and ripen best
Neighbored by fruit of baser quality.
1.1.60-63.

O, let their bodies follow after, my dear liege,
With blood and sword and fire to win your right!
1.1.130-131.

Therefore doth heaven divide the state of man in divers functions, setting endeavour in continual motion
1.1.182-185.

Either our history shall with full mouth
speak freely of our acts, or else our grave
1.1.230-231.

Therefore let every man now task his thought
that this fair action may on foot be brought.
1.1.308-309.

Things must be as they may.
2.1.21.

Though patience be a tired mare, yet she will plod.
2.1.24.

An oath of mickle might; and fury shall abate.
2.1.64.

Base is the slave that pays.

2.1.93.

If little faults proceeding on distemper shall not be winked at, how shall we stretch our eye when capital crimes, chewed, swallowed, and digested, appear before us?
2.2.54-57.

Oaths are straws.
2.3.51.

I desire nothing but odds with England
2.3.128-129.

Now he weighs time even to the utmost grain.
2.3.137-138.

In case of defense 'tis best to weigh
the enemy more might than he seems.
2.4.43-44.

Self-love, my liege, is not so vile a sin as self-neglecting.
2.4.72.

In peace there's nothing so becomes a man
as modest stillness and humility;
But when the blast of war blows in our ears,
then imitate the action of the tiger;
stiffen the sinews, summon up the blood,
disguise fair nature with hard-favour'd rage;
then lend the eye a terrible aspect;
Let it pry through the portage of the head
like the brass cannon: let the brow o'erwhelm it
as fearfully as doth a galled rock
O'erhang and jutty his confounded base,
Swill'd with the wild and wasteful ocean.
3.1.3-14.

I would give all my fame for a pot of ale and safety.
3.2.11.

They will steal anything and call it a purchase.

3.2.37.

What rein can hold licentious wickedness when down the hill he holds his fierce career?
3.3.22-23.

Let man go free.
3.6.41.

The earth sings when he touches it.
3.7.17.

There is flattery in friendship.
3.7.113.

Give the devil his due.
3.7.114.

Foolish curs, that run winking into the mouth of a Russian bear, and have their heads crush'd like rotten apples! You may as well say that's a valiant flea that dare eat his breakfast in the lip of a lion.
3.7.139-142.

We are in great danger; the greater therefore should our courage be.
4.1.1-2.

There is some soul of goodness in things evil,
would men observingly distil it out;
for our bad neighbor makes us early stirrers,
which is both healthful and good husbandry.
4.1.5-8.

When the mind is quick'ned, out of doubt
the organs, though defunct and dead before,
break up their drowsy grave and newly move
with casted slough and fresh legerity.
4.1.20-23.

There are few die well that die in battle.
4.1.141.

Every subjects duty is the King's; but ever subject's soul is his own.
4.1.175-176.

O, God of battles, steel my soldier's hearts,
possess them not with fear!
4.1.285-286.

There is not work enough for all our hands.
4.2.19.

He is as full of valour as of kindnesss;
Princely in both.
4.3.15-16.

If it be a sin to covet honour,
I am the most offending soul alive.
4.3.28-29.

He today that sheds his blood with me shall be my brother.
4.3.61-62.

All things are ready, if our minds be so.
4.3.71.

Let life be short, else shame will be too long.
4.4.23.

As I suck blood, I will some mercy show.
4.4.63.

The empty vessel makes the greatest sound.
4.4.67.

I was not angry since I came to France
until this instant.
4.7.51-52.

That's a lie in thy throat.
4.8.15.

Take it, God,

For it is none but thine.
4.8.108-109.

You have witchcraft in your lips.
5.1.271.

Nice customs curtsy to great kings.
5.2.266.

Love is blind.
5.2.295.

HENRY VI PART 1

Too famous to live long.
1.1.6.

If Henry were recall'd to life again, this news would cause him once more to yield the ghost.
1.1.65-66.

Salisbury is a desperate homicide;
Hei fighteth as one weary of his life.
The other lords, like lions wanting food,
Do rush upon us as their hungry prey.
1.2.25-28.

Lean, raw-bon'd rascals!
1.2.35.

These women are shrewd tempters with their tongues.
1.2.123.

Glory is like a circle in the water,
Which never ceaseth to enlarge itself
Till by broad spreading it disperse to nought.
1.2.133-135.

Bright star of Venus, falln'd down on the earth,
How may I reverently worship thee enough?
1.2.144-145.

Guard thy head,
For I intend to have it ere long.
1.3.86-87.

Heavens, can you suffer hell so to prevail?

My breast I'll burst with straining of my courage,
And from my shoulders crack my arms asunder,
But I will chastise this high-minded strumpet.
1.4.9-12.

My thoughts are whirled like a potters wheel;
I know not where I am nor what I do.
1.5.18-19.

When a world of men
Could not prevail with all their oratory,
Yet hath a woman's kindness overrul'd.
2.2.48-50.

Unbidden guests are often welcomest when they are gone.
2.2.55-56.

The plot is laid. If all things fall out right,
I shall as famous be by this exploit
As Scythian Tamyris by Cyrus' death.
2.3.5-7.

Thy mirth shall turn to moan.
2.3.44.

The truth appears so naked on my side
that any purblind eye may find it out.
2.4.19-20.

Go forward, and be chok'd with thy ambition!
2.4.111.

First, lean thine agèd back against mine arm,
And in that ease I'll tell thee my disease.
2.5.43-44.

Civil dissension is a viperous worm
that gnaws the bowels of the commonwealth.
3.1.72-73.

The presence of a king endgenders love
Amongst his subjects and his loyal friends,

As it disanimates his enemies.
3.1.81-183.

As fest'red members rot but by degree,
till bones and flesh and sines fall away,
so will this base and envious discord breed.
3.1.192-194.

O, let no words, but dees, revenge this treason!
3.2.49.

Undaunted spirit in a dying breast.
3.2.98.
They that of late were daring with their scoffs
Are glad and fain by flight to save themselves.
3.2.113-114.

Kings and mightiest potentates must die,
for that's the end of human misery.
3.2.136-137.

Care is no cure, but rather corrosive,
for things that are not to be remedied.
3.3.3-4.

Strike those that hurt, and hurt not those that help.
3.3.54.

When thou shalt see I'll meet thee to thy cost.
3.4.43.

Let us not forgo
That for a trifle that was bought with blood.
4.1.149-150.

When envy breeds unkind division;
there comes the ruin, there begins confusion.
4.1.193-194.

I always thought
It was both impious and unnatural

That such immunity and bloody strife
Should reign among the professors of one thing.
5.1.11-14.

A goodly prize, fit for the devil's grace.
5.3.33.

She is a woman, therefore to be won.
5.3.79.

To be a queen in bondage is more vile
than is a slave in base servility.
5.3.112-113.

This argues what her kind of life hath been—
Wicked and vile; so her death concludes.
5.4.15-16.

Because you want the grace that others have,
you judge it straight a thing impossible
to compass wonders but by help of devils.
5.4.46-48.

I'll rather keep that which I have than, coveting for more,
be cast from possibility of all.
5.4.144-146.

Marriage is a matter of more worth
than to be dealt in by attorneyship.
5.5.55-56.

What is wedlock forced but a hell, an age of discord and continual strife?
5.5.63-64.

HENRY VI PART 2

O lord, that lends me life,
Lend me a heart replete with thankfulness!
1.1.19-20.

And, being a woman, I will not be slack
To play my part in fortune's pageant.
1.2.66-67.

To see how God in all his creatures works!
2.1.7.

'tis but a base and ignoble mind
That mount no higher than a bird can soar.
2.1.13-14.

O God, what mischiefs work the wicked ones,
heaping confusion on their own heads thereby!
2.1.181-182.

They hold by force, and not by right.
2.2.30.

God shall be my hope,
my stay, my guide, and lantern to my feet.
2.3.23-24.

God defend the right.
2.3.55.

Teach me not to forget myself!
2.4.27.

Small curs are not regarded when they grin,
but great men tremble when the lion roars

3.1.18-19.

Seems he a dove? His feathers are but borrowed,
For he's disposèd as the hateful raven.
Is he a lamb? His skin is surely lent him,
For he's inclined as is the ravenous wolves.
Who cannot steal a shape that means deceit?
3.1.76-80.

A heart unspotted in not easily daunted.
3.1.100.

Be that thou hop'st to be; or what thou art
resign to death-- it is not worth th' enjoying.
3.1.333-334.

Virtue is chok'd with foul ambition,
And charity chas'd hence, by rancour's hand
3.1.143-144.

Ah, thus King Henry throws away his crutch
Before his legs be firm to bear his body.
3.1.189-190.

Wer't not madness then,
To make the fox surveyor of the fold?
3.1.253-254.

My brain, more busy than the laboring spider,
Weaves tedious snares to trap mine enemies.
Well, nobles, well, 'tis politicly done
To send me packing with an host of men.
3.1.339-343.

O, let the vile world end
And the promised flames of the last day
Knit earth and heaven together!
3.2.40-42.

We were but hollow friends.
3.2.66.

Would curses kill, as doth the mandrake's groan,
I would invent as bitter searching terms,
As curst, as harsh, and horrible to hear,
Delivered strongly through my fixèd teeth,
With full as many signs of deadly hate,
As lean-faced Envy in her loathsome cave.
3.2.320-325.

If I depart from thee I cannot live.
3.2.388.

So bad a death argues a monstrous life.
3.3.30.

Forbear to judge, for we are sinners all.
3.3.31.

Even thus two friends condemned
Embrace and kiss and take ten thousand leaves,
Loather a hundred times to part than die.
3.3.353-355.

Wedded be thou to the hags of hell.
4.1.79.

Small things make base men proud.
4.1.106.

It is impossible that I should die
by such a lowly vassal as thyself.
4.1.110-111.

True nobility is exempt from fear.
4.1.129.

Thou hast hit it; for there's no better sign of a brave mind than a hard hand.
4.2.18.

The first thing we do, let's kill all the lawyers.
4.2.72.

Is not this a lamentable thing, that of the skin of an innocent lamb should be made parchment; that parchment, being scribbled o'er, should undo a man?
4.2.74-75.

Can he that speaks with the tongue of an enemy be a good councillor, or no?
4.2.165-166.

For Go forbid so many simple souls
Should perish by the sword!
4.4.10-11.

O graceless men! They know not what they do.
4.4.38.

The trust I have is in mine innocence,
And therefore am I bold and resolute.
4.4.59-60.

And here, sitting
upon London Stone, I charge and command
that, of the city's cost, the Pissing Conduit run
nothing but claret wine this first year of our reign.
4.6.1-5.

Thou hast most traitorously corrupted the youth of the realm in erecting a grammar school; and whereas, before, our forefathers had no other books but the score and the tally, thou hast caused printing to be us'd, and, contrary to the King, his crown, and Dignity, thou hast built a paper-mill.
4.6.25-30.

The proudest peer in the realm shall not wear a head on his shoulders, unless he pay me tribute
4.6.113.

Thou hast
most traitorously corrupted the youth of the realm
in erecting a grammar school; and whereas,
before, our forefathers had no other books but the
score and the tally, thou hast caused printing to be
used, and, contrary to the King his crown and dignity,
thou hast built a paper mill. It will be proved
to thy face that thou hast men about thee that usually
talk of a noun and a verb and such abominable
words as no Christian ear can endure to hear.
Thou hast appointed justices of peace to call poor
men before them about matters they were not able
to answer. Moreover, thou hast put them in prison;
and, because they could not read, thou hast
hanged them, when indeed only for that cause
they have been most worthy to live.
4.7.31-43.

Was never subject long'd to be a king
As I do long and wish to be a subject.
4.9.5-6.

How much thou wrong'st me, heaven be my judge.
Die, damned wretch, the curse of her that bare thee!
4.10.75-76.

If not in heaven, you'll surely sup in hell.
5.1.216.

Sword, hold thy temper; heart, be wrathfull still;
Priests pray for enemies, but princes kill.
5.2.71.

And like rich hangings in a homely house,

So was his will in his old feeble body.
5.3.12-13.

HENRY VI PART 3

A woman's general; what should we fear?
1.2.68.

Would I had died a maid
And never seen thee, never borne thee son,
Seeing thou hast prov'd so unnatural a father!
1.1.216-218.

But for a kingdom any oath may be broken.
I would break a thousand oaths to rein one year.
1.2.15-16.

Do but think how sweet a thing it is to wear a crown.
1.3.28-29.

Cowards fight when they can fly no farther
1.4.40.

It is war's prize to take all vantages;
and ten to one is no impeach of honour.
1.4.59-60.

That beggars mounted run their horse to death.
1.4.127.

'Tis beauty that doth oft make women proud.
1.4.128.

Women are soft, mild, pitiful, and flexible.
1.4.141.

To weep is to make less the depth of grief.
2.1.85.

The smallest worm will turn, being troddenon.

And doves will peck in safeguard of their brood.
2.2.17-18.

Unreasonable creatures feed their young.
2.2.26.

Didst thou never hear that things ill got had ever bad success?
2.2.46.

Who should succeed the father but the son?
2.3.93.

Why stand we like soft-hearted women here,
wailing our losses, whiles the foe doth rage,
and look upon, as if the tragedy were play'd in jest by counterfeiting actors?
2.3.25-28.

This battle fares like to the morning's war,
when dying clouds contend with growing light,
what time the shepherd, blowing of his nails,
can neither call it perfect day nor night.
Now sways it this way, like a mighty sea
forced by the tide to combat with the wind;
now sways it that way, like the selfsame sea
forced to retire by fury of the wind:
sometime the flood prevails, and then the wind;
now one the better, then another best;
both tugging to be victors, breast to breast,
yet neither conqueror nor conquered:
so is the equal of this fell war.
Here on this molehill will I sit me down.
To whom God will, there be the victory!
2.5.1-15.

O God! methinks it were a happy life,
to be no better than a homely swain;
to sit upon a hill, as I do now,
to carve out dials quaintly, point by point,
thereby to see the minutes how they run,
how many make the hour full complete;

how many hours bring about the day;
how many days will finish up the year;
how many years a mortal man may live.
When this is known, then to divide the times:
so many hours must I tend my flock;
so many hours must I take my rest;
so many hours must I contemplate;
so many hours must I sport myself;
so many days my ewes have been with young;
so many weeks ere the poor fools will ean:
so many years ere I shall shear the fleece:
so minutes, hours, days, months, and years,
pass'd over to the end they were created,
would bring white hairs unto a quiet grave.
2.5.21-40.

Ah, what a life were this! how sweet! how lovely!
gives not the hawthorn-bush a sweeter shade
to shepherds looking on their silly sheep,
than doth a rich embroider'd canopy
to kings that fear their subjects' treachery?
O, yes, it doth; a thousand-fold it doth.
2.5.41-46.

Ill blows the wind that profits nobody.
2.5.55.

Pardon me, God, I knew not what I did.
2.5.69.

Whiles lions war and battle for their dens,
poor harmless lambs abide their enmity.
2.5.74-75.

O boy, thy father gave thee life too soon,
and hath bereft thee of thy life too late!
2.5.93-94.

What doth cherish weeds but gentle air?
2.6.21.

What makes robbery bold but too much lenity?
2.6.22.

Measure for measure must be answered.
2.6.55.

The tiger will be mild whiles she doth mourn.
3.1.39.

Men may talk of kings, and why not I?
3.1.58.

My crown is called content;
a crown it is that seldom kings enjoy.
3.1.64-65.

King Edward: To tell you plain, I am to lie with thee.
Lady Grey: To tell you plain, I had rather lie in prison.
3.2.69-70.

'Tis a happy thing to be the father unto many sons.
3.2.104-105.

Why, I can smile, and murder whiles I smile
3.2.182.

How mischance hath trod my title down
and with dishonour laid me on the ground.
3.3.8-9.

Impatience waiteth on true sorrow
3.3.42.

How can tyrants safely govern home
unless abroad they purchase great alliance?
3.3.69-70.

Time suppresseth wrongs.
3.3.77.

His love was an eternal plant
whereof the root was fix'd in virtues ground.
3.3.124-125.

I was the chief that rais'd him to the crown
and I'll be the chief that bring him down again.
3.3.263-264.

Yet hasty marriage seldom proveth well.
4.1.18.

Tis better using France than trusting France.
4.1.42.

Though fortune's malice overthrow my state,
my mind exceeds the compass of her wheel.
4.3.46-47.

I hear, yet say not much, but think the more.
4.1.83.

Better do so than tarry and be hang'd.
4.5.26.

Caged birds...
after many moody thoughts,
at last notes of household harmony
they quite forget their loss of liberty.
4.6.12-15.

His head by nature fram'd to wear a crown,
his hand to wield a sceptre; and himself
likely in time to bless a regal throne.
4.6.71-73.

When the box hath once got his nose,
he'll soon find means to make the body follow.
4.7.25-26.

My pity hath been balm to heal their wounds,
my mildness hath allay'd their swelling griefs,
my mercy dried their water-flowering tears;
I have not been desirous of their wealth,
nor much oppress'd them with great subsidies,

nor forward of revenge, though they much err'd.
then why should they love Edward more than me?
4.8.41-47.

The harder match'd, the greater victory.
5.1.70.

That I must yield my body to the earth,
and, by my fall, the conquest to my foe.
5.2.9-10.

Why, what is pomp, rule, reign, but earth and dust?
and live how we can, yet die we must.
5.2.27-28.

But in the midst of this bright-shining day,
I spy a black, suspicious, threatening cloud
5.3.3-4.

Wise men ne'er sit and wail their loss,
but cheerly seek how to redress their harms.
5.4.1-2.

'Tis sin to flatter.
5.5.3.

Thou wast born to be a plague to men.
5.5.28.

Men ne'er spend their fury on a child.
5.5.57.

What's worse than murder, that I may name it?
5.5.58.

Butchers and villains; bloody cannibals.
5.5.61.

Suspicion always haunts the guilty mind.
5.6.11.

'Twas sin before, but now 'tis charity.

5.5.76.

My breast can better brook thy dagger's point
than can my ears that tragic history.
5.6.27.

So first the harmless sheep doth yield his fleece,
and next his throat unto the butchers knife.
5.6.8-9.

Thus have we swept suspicion from our seat
and made our footstool of security.
5.7.13-14

RICHARD III

Why, thus it is when men are rul'd by women
1.1.62

The readiest way to make the wench amends
is to become her husband and her father
1.1.155-156.

And mortal eyes cannot endure the devil
1.2.45.

thou hast made the happy Earth thy hell
1.2.52.

Blush, blush, thou lump of foul deformity.
1.2.57.

G, which renders good for bad, blessings for curses.
1.2.69.

Fouler than heart can think thee, thou canst' make
no excuse current but to hang thyself
1.2.84-83.

Your beauty that did haunt me in my sleep
to undertake the death of all the world
so I might live on hour in your sweet bosom.
1.2.122-124.

His better doth not breathe upon the earth.
1.2.140.

Though I wish thy death,
I will not be thy executioner.
1.2.184-185.

Shine out, fair sun, till I have bought a glass,
that I may see my shadow as I pass.
1.2.262-263.

Hie thee to hell for shame and leave this world
1.3.142.

Can curses pierce the clouds and enter heaven?
Why then, give way, dull clouds, to my quick curses!
1.3.194-195.

They that stand high have many blasts that shake them,
and if they fall they dash themselves to pieces.
1.3.260-261.

Have not to do with him, beware of him
sin, death, and hell, have set their marks on him,
and all their ministers attend on him.
1.3.292-294.

And thus I clothe my naked villainy
with odd old ends stolen forth of holy writ,
and seem a saint when most I play the devil.
1.3.337-339.

Princes have but their titles for their glories,
and outward honour for an inward toil;
and for unfelt imaginations
they often feel a world of restless cares,
so that between their titles and low name,
there's nothing differs but the outward fame.
1.4.78-83.

Are you drawn forth among a world of men
To slay the innocent?
1.4.176-177.

They that set you on
To do this deed will hate you for the deed.
1.4.252-253.

Ah, that deceit should steal such gentle shape,
and with a virtuous vizor hide deep vice!
2.2.27-28.

I'll join with black despair against my soul
and to myself become an enemy.
2.2.36-37.

I am your sorrow's nurse,
and will pamper it with lamentation.
2.2.87-88.

All of us have cause
to wail the dimming of our shining star;
but none can help our harms by wailing them.
2.2.101-103.

Truly, the hearts of men are full of fear.
You cannot reason almost with a man
That looks not heavily and full of dread.
2.3.38-40.

Small herbs have pace; great weeds do grow apace.
2.4.13.

Nor more can you distinguish of a man
Than of his outward show, which, God he knows,
Seldom or never jumpeth with the heart.
3.1.9-11.

Not for all this land would I be guilty of so deep a sin.
3.1.42-43.

So wise so young, they say, do never live long.
3.1.79.

His wit set down to make his valour live,
Death makes no conquest of this conqueror;
For now he lives in fame thou not in life.
3.1.86-88.

Short summers lightly have a forward spring.

3.1.94.

God bless the prince from all the pack of you!
3.3.5.

We know each others faces; for our hearts,
he knows no more of mine than I of yours.
3.4.10-11.

Three times today my foot-cloth horse did stumble,
and started when he look'd upon the Tower,
as loath to bear me to the slaughterhouse.
3.4.86-88.

Bad is the world; and all will come to nought,
when such ill dealing must be seen in thought.
3.6.13-14.

Death and destruction dog thee at thy heels.
4.1.40.

Repays he my deep service with such contempt?
4.2.123.

We must be brief when traitors brave the field
4.1.57.

So now prosperity begins to mellow
And drop into the rotten mouth of death.
4.4.1-2.

Cancel his bond of life, dear God, I pray,
That I may live and say, "The dog is dead".
4.4.77-78.

From forth the kennel of thy wound hath crept
a hell-hound that doth hunt us all to death.
4.4.47-48.

The foul defacer of Gods handiwork.
4.4.52.

Why should calamity be full of words?

4.4.126.

Thou cam'st on earth to make the earth my hell.
4.4.166.

Bloody thou art; bloody will be thy end.
4.4.194.

No doubt the murderous knife was dull and blunt
Till it was whetted on thy stone-hard heart.
4.1.226-227.

Plain and honest is too harsh a style.
4.4.360.

I never was nor never will be false.
4.4.495.

Let not our babbling dreams affright our souls.
Conscience is but a word that cowards use,
Devised at first to keep the strong in awe.
Our strong arms be our conscience, swords our law.
March on. Join bravely. Let us to it pell mell,
If not to heaven, then hand in hand to hell.
5.3.309-314.

I have set my life upon a cast
and I will stand the hazard of the die.
5.4.9-10.

A horse! A horse! My kingdom for a horse!
5.4.13.

HENRY THE VIII

A man may weep upon his wedding day.
Prologue; 32.

I wonder that such a keech can with his very bulk
Take up the rays o' th' beneficial sun,
And keep it from the earth.
1.1.54-56.

I can see his pride
Peep through each part of him.
1.1.68-69.

A beggar's book
outworths a nobles blood.
1.1.123-124.

To climb steep hills
requires slow pace at first.
1.1.131-132.
Anger is like
A full hot horse, who being allo'd his way,
Self-mettle tires him.
1.1.133-135.

Know you not
The fire that mounts the liquor till't run o'er
Is seeming to augment it wastes it?
1.1.143-145.

The will of heav'n
be done in this and all things.
1.1.209-210.

This makes bold mouths.
Tongues spit their duties out, and cold hearts freeze
Allegiance in them. Their curses now
Live where their prayers did; and it's come to pass
This tractable obedience is a slave
To each incensèd will.
1.2.60-65.

If we shall stand still,
in fear our motion will be mock'd or carp'd at,
we should take root here where we sit, or sit
state-statutes only.
1.2.85-87.

When these so noble benefits shall prove
Not well dispos'd, the mind growing once corrupt,
They turn to vicious forms, ten time more ugly
Than ever they were fair.
1.2.115-118.

On my soul, I'll speak but the truth.
1.2.177.

There's mischief in this man.
1.2.187.

If he may find mercy in the law, 'tis his; if none,
let him not seek't of us.
1.2.211-213.

Good company, good wine, good welcome,
Can make good people.
1.3.6-7.

That churchman bears a bounteous mind indeed,
a hand as fruitful as the land that feeds us;
his dews fall everywhere.
1.3.55-57.

Two women placed together makes cold weather.

1.4.22.

Even as the axe falls, if I be not faithful!
the law I bear no malice for my death.
2.1.61-62.

I as free forgive you
As I would be forgiven. I forgive all.
2.1.82-83.

Yet I am richer than my basic accusers
That never knew what truth meant.
2.1.104-105.

Verily,
I swear 'tis better to be lowly born
and range with humble livers in content
than to be perk'd up in a glist'ring grief
and wear a golden sorrow.
2.3.18-22.

Honour's train
is longer than his foreskirt.
2.3.97-98.

Beauty and honour in her are so mingled
That they have caught the king.
2.4.76-77.

They vex me past my patience.
2.4.130.

That man I' th' world who shall report he has
A better wife, let him in nought be tursted
For speaking false in that.
2.4.133-136.

I must tell you you tender more your persons' honour than your high profession spiritual.
2.4.115-117.

WILLIAM SHAKESPEARE

Would all other women
Could speak this with as free as soul as I do.
3.1.21-22.

All hoods make not monks.
3.1.23.

Truth loves open dealing.
3.1.39.

Ye have angels faces', but heaven knows your hearts.
3.1.145.

A noble spirit, as yours was put into you, ever casts
such doubts as false coin from it.
3.1.169-171.

She is a gallant creature, and complete
in mind an feature.
3.2.49-51.

My endeavours,
I have ever come too short of my desires.
3.2.169-170.

Though perils did
abound as thick as thought could make 'em, and
appear in forms more horrid-- yet my duty,
as doth a rock against he chiding flood,
should the approach of this wild river break,
and stand unshaken yours.
3.2.194-198.

Now I feel
Of what course metal ye are moulded.
3.2.238-239.

So farewell to the little good you bear me.
3.2.350.

O, how wretched is that poor man that hangs on princes' favours!

3.2.367.

Fling away ambition:
by that sin fell the angels; how can man, then,
the image of his Maker, hope to win by it?
love thyself last: cherish those hearts that hate thee;
corruption wins not more than honesty.
still in thy right hand carry gentle peace,
to silence envious tongues. Be just, and fear not:
let all the ends thou aim'st at be thy country's,
thy God's, and truth's;
3.2.440-448.

I have a soul, and she is an angel.
4.1.44.

He was a man of unbounded stomach,
Ever ranking himself with princes.
4.2.33-34.

If heaven had pleas'd to have given me longer life
and ale means, we had not parted thus.
4.2.152-153.

Men's evil manners live in brass; their virtues
we write in water.
4.2.45-46.

That comfort comes too late,
'tis like a pardon after execution.
4.2.120-121.

Affairs that walk--
as they say spirits do-- at midnight have
in them a wilder nature than the business
that seeks despatch'd by day.
5.1.13-16.

He's a rank weed, Sir Thomas,
And we most root him out.
5.1.53-54.

The good I stand on is my truth and honesty;
I they shall fail, I with mine enemies
Will triumph over my person.
5.1.122-124.

I fear nothing what can be said against me.
5.1.125-126.

He has strangled his language in his tears.
5.1.157.

We all are men,
In our own natures frail and capable
of our flesh.
5.2.10-12.

'tis cruelty to load a falling man.
5.3.76-77.

I told ye all,
When we first put this dangerous stone ar-rolling,
'twould fall upon ourselves.
5.3.103-105.

SOLILOQUIES

Shakespeare's greatest monolgues- spoken alone or in the company of another character- build stories, explain psychology, and touch a part of us. We understand how other characters feel; we see a part of us or someone we know expressed in Shakespeare's words. There are many monologues in many plays, but few soliloquies that match the greatness of Shakespeare's.

Here are Shakespeare's greatest soliloquies, as measured by scope, style or both. Famous and brilliant, the Bard's soliloquies speak to us now as they have done so for 300 years.

I've listed the characters who spoke the lines to help readers to be informed and provide a bit of context to the words. If there is no character listed, the speaker is the title character.

All the world's a stage,
And all the men and women merely players;
They have their exits and their entrances,
And one man in his time plays many parts,
His acts being seven ages. At first the infant,
Mewling and puking in the nurse's arms.
Then, the whining school-boy with his satchel
And shining morning face, creeping like snail
Unwillingly to school. And then the lover,
Sighing like furnace, with a woeful ballad

Made to his mistress' eyebrow. Then, a soldier,
Full of strange oaths, and bearded like the pard,
Jealous in honour, sudden, and quick in quarrel,
Seeking the bubble reputation
Even in the cannon's mouth. And then, the justice,
In fair round belly, with a good capon lined,
With eyes severe, and beard of formal cut,
Full of wise saws, and modern instances,
And so he plays his part. The sixth age shifts
Into the lean and slippered pantaloon,
With spectacles on nose and pouch on side,
His youthful hose, well saved, a world too wide
For his shrunk shank, and his big manly voice,
Turning again toward childish treble, pipes
And whistles in his sound. Last scene of all,
That ends this strange eventful history,
Is second childishness and mere oblivion,
Sans teeth, sans eyes, sans taste, sans everything.
Jacques- As You Like It. 2.4.139-166.

Go play, boy, play. Thy mother plays, and I
play too, but so disgraced a part, whose issue
will hiss me to my grave. Contempt and clamor
will be my knell. Go play, boy, play.—There have been,
or I am much deceived, cuckolds ere now;
and many a man there is, even at this present,
now while I speak this, holds his wife by th' arm,
that little thinks she has been sluiced in 's absence,
and his pond fished by his next neighbor, by
Sir Smile, his neighbor. Nay, there's comfort in 't
whiles other men have gates and those gates
opened, as mine, against their will. Should all despair
that have revolted wives, the tenth of mankind
would hang themselves. Physic for 't there's none.
It is a bawdy planet, that will strike
Where 'tis predominant; and 'tis powerful, think it,
from east, west, north, and south. Be it concluded,
no barricado for a belly. Know 't,

it will let in and out the enemy
with bag and baggage. Many thousand on 's
have the disease and feel 't not.—How now, boy?
Leontes- The Winter's Tale; 1.1.185-207.

To bait fish withal; if it will feed nothing else,
it will feed my revenge. He hath disgraced me and
hindered me half a million, laughed at my losses,
mocked at my gains, scorned my nation, thwarted
my bargains, cooled my friends, heated mine enemies—
and what's his reason? I am a Jew. Hath not
a Jew eyes? Hath not a Jew hands, organs, dimensions,
senses, affections, passions? Fed with the
same food, hurt with the same weapons, subject to
the same diseases, healed by the same means,
warmed and cooled by the same winter and summer
as a Christian is? If you prick us, do we not
bleed? If you tickle us, do we not laugh? If you
poison us, do we not die? And if you wrong us, shall
we not revenge? If we are like you in the rest, we will
resemble you in that. If a Jew wrong a Christian,
what is his humility? Revenge. If a Christian wrong
a Jew, what should his sufferance be by Christian
example? Why, revenge! The villainy you teach me I
will execute, and it shall go hard but I will better the
instruction.
Shylock- The Merchant of Venice; 3.1.45-62.

To be or not to be—that is the question:
whether 'tis nobler in the mind to suffer
the slings and arrows of outrageous fortune,
or to take arms against a sea of troubles
and, by opposing, end them. To die, to sleep—
no more—and by a sleep to say we end
The heartache and the thousand natural shocks

that flesh is heir to—'tis a consummation
devoutly to be wished. To die, to sleep—
to sleep, perchance to dream. Ay, there's the rub,
for in that sleep of death what dreams may come,
when we have shuffled off this mortal coil,
must give us pause. There's the respect
that makes calamity of so long life.
For who would bear the whips and scorns of time,
th' oppressor's wrong, the proud man's contumely,
the pangs of despised love, the law's delay,
the insolence of office, and the spurns
that patient merit of th' unworthy takes,
when he himself might his quietus make
with a bare bodkin? Who would fardels bear,
to grunt and sweat under a weary life,
but that the dread of something after death,
the undiscovered country from whose bourn
no traveler returns, puzzles the will
and makes us rather bear those ills we have
than fly to others that we know not of?
thus conscience does make cowards ⟨of us all,⟩
Hamlet; 3.1.56-83.

Thou, Nature, art my goddess. To thy law
My services are bound. Wherefore should I
Stand in the plague of custom, and permit
The curiosity of nations to deprive me
For that I am some twelve or fourteen moonshines
Lag of a brother? why "bastard"? Wherefore "base,"
When my dimensions are as well compact,
My mind as generous and my shape as true
As honest madam's issue? Why brand they us
With "base," with "baseness," "bastardy," "base," "base,"
Who, in the lusty stealth of nature, take
More composition and fierce quality
Than doth within a dull, stale, tired bed

Go to th' creating a whole tribe of fops
Got 'tween asleep and wake? Well then,
Legitimate Edgar, I must have your land.
Our father's love is to the bastard Edmund
As to th' legitimate. Fine word, "legitimate."
Well, my legitimate, if this letter speed
And my invention thrive, Edmund the base
Shall th' legitimate. I grow, I prosper.
Now, gods, stand up for bastards!
Edmund- King Lear; 2.1.1-22.

O, reason not the need! Our basest beggars
Are in the poorest thing superfluous.
Allow not nature more than nature needs,
Man's life is cheap as beast's. Thou art a lady;
If only to go warm were gorgeous,
Why, nature needs not what thou gorgeous wear'st,
Which scarcely keeps thee warm. But, for true need—
You heavens, give me that patience, patience I need!
You see me here, you gods, a poor old man
As full of grief as age, wretched in both.
If it be you that stirs these daughters' hearts
Against their father, fool me not so much
To bear it tamely. Touch me with noble anger,
And let not women's weapons, water drops,
Stain my man's cheeks.—No, you unnatural hags,
I will have such revenges on you both
That all the world shall—I will do such things—
What they are yet I know not, but they shall be
The terrors of the Earth! You think I'll weep.
No, I'll not weep.
I have full cause of weeping, but this heart
Shall break into a hundred thousand flaws
Or ere I'll weep.—O Fool, I shall go mad!
King Lear; 2.4.263-285.
She should have died hereafter;

WILLIAMSHAKESPEARE

There would have been a time for such a word.
To-morrow and to-morrow and to-morrow,
Creeps in this petty pace from day to day
To the last syllable of recorded time,
And all our yesterday shave lighted fools
The way to dusty death. Out, out, brief candle!
Life's but a walking shadow, a poor player,
That struts and frets his hour upon the stage,
And then is heard no more; it is a tale
Told by an idiot, full of sound and fury,
Signifying nothing.
Macbeth; 5.5.17.

Friends, Romans, countrymen, lend me your ears.
I come to bury Caesar, not to praise him.
The evil that men do lives after them;
The good is oft interrèd with their bones.
So let it be with Caesar. The noble Brutus
Hath told you Caesar was ambitious.
If it were so, it was a grievous fault,
And grievously hath Caesar answered it.
Here, under leave of Brutus and the rest
(For Brutus is an honorable man;
So are they all, all honorable men),
Come I to speak in Caesar's funeral.
He was my friend, faithful and just to me,
But Brutus says he was ambitious,
And Brutus is an honorable man.
He hath brought many captives home to Rome,
Whose ransoms did the general coffers fill.
Did this in Caesar seem ambitious?
When that the poor have cried, Caesar hath wept;
Ambition should be made of sterner stuff.
Marc Antony- Julius Caesar; 3.2.72-101.

What is here?
Gold? Yellow, glittering, precious gold?

No, gods, I am no idle votarist.
Roots, you clear heavens!
Thus much of this will make
Black white, foul fair, wrong right,
Base noble, old young, coward valiant.
Ha, you gods! Why this? What this, you gods? Why, this
Will lug your priests and servants from your sides,
Pluck stout men's pillows from below their heads.
This yellow slave
Will knit and break religions, bless th' accursed,
Make the hoar leprosy adored, place thieves
And give them title, knee, and approbation
With senators on the bench.
Timon of Athens; 4.3.26-37.

If there were reason for these miseries,
Then into limits could I bind my woes.
When heaven doth weep, doth not the Earth o'erflow?
If the winds rage, doth not the sea wax mad,
Threat'ning the welkin with his big-swoll'n face?
And wilt thou have a reason for this coil?
I am the sea. Hark how her sighs doth flow!
She is the weeping welkin, I the Earth.
Then must my sea be movèd with her sighs;
Then must my Earth with her continual tears
Become a deluge, overflowed and drowned,
For why my bowels cannot hide her woes
But like a drunkard must I vomit them.
Then give me leave, for losers will have leave
To ease their stomachs with their bitter tongues.
Titus Andronicus; 3.1.223-238.

Tis not due yet; I would be loath to pay him before
his day. What need I be so forward with him that
calls not on me? Well, 'tis no matter; honour pricks
me on. Yea, but how if honour prick me off when I
come on? how then? Can honour set to a leg? no: or

an arm? no: or take away the grief of a wound? no.
Honour hath no skill in surgery, then? no. What is
honour? a word. What is in that word honour? what
is that honour? air. A trim reckoning! Who hath it?
he that died o' Wednesday. Doth he feel it? no.
Doth he hear it? no. 'Tis insensible, then. Yea,
to the dead. But will it not live with the living?
no. Why? detraction will not suffer it. Therefore
I'll none of it. Honour is a mere scutcheon: and so
ends my catechism.
Falstaff; Henry the IV part 1: 5.1.127-139

This day is called the feast of Crispian:
He that outlives this day, and comes safe home,
Will stand a tip-toe when the day is named,
And rouse him at the name of Crispian.
He that shall live this day, and see old age,
Will yearly on the vigil feast his neighbours,
And say 'To-morrow is Saint Crispian:'
Then will he strip his sleeve and show his scars.
And say 'These wounds I had on Crispin's day.'
Old men forget: yet all shall be forgot,
But he'll remember with advantages
What feats he did that day: then shall our names.
Familiar in his mouth as household words
Harry the king, Bedford and Exeter,
Warwick and Talbot, Salisbury and Gloucester,
Be in their flowing cups freshly remember'd.
This story shall the good man teach his son;
And Crispin Crispian shall ne'er go by,
From this day to the ending of the world,
But we in it shall be remember'd;
We few, we happy few, we band of brothers;
For he to-day that sheds his blood with me
Shall be my brother; be he ne'er so vile,
This day shall gentle his condition:
And gentlemen in England now a-bed

Shall think themselves accursed they were not here,
And hold their manhoods cheap whiles any speaks
That fought with us upon Saint Crispin's day.
Henry the V; 4.3.40-67.
O God! methinks it were a happy life,
to be no better than a homely swain;
to sit upon a hill, as I do now,
to carve out dials quaintly, point by point,
thereby to see the minutes how they run,
how many make the hour full complete;
how many hours bring about the day;
how many days will finish up the year;
how many years a mortal man may live.
When this is known, then to divide the times:
so many hours must I tend my flock;
so many hours must I take my rest;
so many hours must I contemplate;
so many hours must I sport myself;
so many days my ewes have been with young;
so many weeks ere the poor fools will ean:
so many years ere I shall shear the fleece:
so minutes, hours, days, months, and years,
pass'd over to the end they were created,
would bring white hairs unto a quiet grave.
King Henry; 2.5.21-40. Henry 6 Part 3.

Now is the winter of our discontent
Made glorious summer by this son of York,
And all the clouds that loured upon our house
In the deep bosom of the ocean buried.
Now are our brows bound with victorious wreaths,
Our bruisèd arms hung up for monuments,
Our stern alarums changed to merry meetings,
Our dreadful marches to delightful measures.
Grim-visaged war hath smoothed his wrinkled front;
And now, instead of mounting barbèd steeds
To fright the souls of fearful adversaries,
He capers nimbly in a lady's chamber

To the lascivious pleasing of a lute.
But I, that am not shaped for sportive tricks,
Nor made to court an amorous looking glass;
I, that am rudely stamped and want love's majesty
To strut before a wanton ambling nymph;
I, that am curtailed of this fair proportion,
Cheated of feature by dissembling nature,
Deformed, unfinished, sent before my time
Into this breathing world scarce half made up,
And that so lamely and unfashionable
That dogs bark at me as I halt by them—
Why, I, in this weak piping time of peace,
Have no delight to pass away the time,
Unless to see my shadow in the sun
And descant on mine own deformity.
And therefore, since I cannot prove a lover
To entertain these fair well-spoken days,
I am determinèd to prove a villain
And hate the idle pleasures of these days.
Plots have I laid, inductions dangerous,
By drunken prophecies, libels, and dreams,
To set my brother Clarence and the King
In deadly hate, the one against the other;
And if King Edward be as true and just
As I am subtle, false, and treacherous,
This day should Clarence closely be mewed up
About a prophecy which says that "G"
Of Edward's heirs the murderer shall be.
Dive, thoughts, down to my soul. Here Clarence comes.
Richard the III; 1.1.1-40.

THE GREAT BIG BOOK OF SHAKESPEARE QUOTES

SONNETS

All of Shakespeare's sonnets are brilliant creations. They consist of fourteen lines of iambic pentameter composed into three quatrains in ABAB rhyme scheme, ending with a rhymed couplet. The sonnets detail different ages of Shakespeare's life, love, and love life, mostly discussing his specific lovers, his changing perspectives and love as a general subject. The sonnets are clever, sometimes cute, sometimes funny, and all artful. Shakespeare's words sail from platonic to erotic, from beautiful to bitter, and everywhere in between. They help paint Shakespeare as a conflicted human, full of passion, brimming with emotion and facing the struggles we all live through.
But are they all universal?
Hardly.
Did Shakespeare's writing lead to greater enlightenment and self-awareness for himself? The analysis has yet to be completed by a psychologist, but I'd wager they did. That alone makes the sonnets worth reading.
More importantly for you us is the question, "Are they univeral enough to illuminate our lives today?" I'd again wager they are, but you will have to read all the sonnets to decide that for yourself. It's worth the effort, if only for the sense of accomplishment.
To begin your journey, here are some of his greatest

sonnets in their entirety as well as the best quotes from the sonnets as body of work. It is impossible to fully separate the emotion of a line from the body of work that sets up the line; but, like a knockout punch, we can recognize the best "hits" in his sonnets. They stand alone as examples of brilliance and artistry.

Not marble, nor the gilded monuments
Of princes, shall outlive this powerful rhyme-
Sonnet 55

Do not kill the spirit of love with a perpetual dullness.
Sonnet 56

So true a fool is love that in your will,
though you do any thing, he thinks no ill.
Sonnet 57

To you it doth belong
Yourself to pardon of self-doing crime.
Sonnet 58

Like as the waves make towards the pebbled shore,
So do our minutes hasten to their end.
Sonnet 60

Since brass, nor stone, nor earth, nor boundless sea,
But sad mortality o'er-sways their power,
How with this rage shall beauty hold a plea,
Whose action is no stronger than a flower?
O, how shall summer's honey breath hold out
Against the wreckful siege of battering days,
When rocks impregnable are not so stout,
Nor gates of steel so strong, but Time decays?
O fearful meditation! where, alack,
Shall Time's best jewel from Time's chest lie hid?
Or what strong hand can hold his swift foot back?

Or who his spoil of beauty can forbid?
　　O, none, unless this miracle have might,
　That in black ink my love may still shine bright.
Sonnet 65

No longer mourn for me when I am dead
Then you shall hear the surly sullen bell
Give warning to the world that I am fled
From this vile world, with vilest worms to dwell:
Nay, if you read this line, remember not
The hand that writ it; for I love you so
That I in your sweet thoughts would be forgot
If thinking on me then should make you woe.
O, if, I say, you look upon this verse
When I perhaps compounded am with clay,
Do not so much as my poor name rehearse.
But let your love even with my life decay,
　　Lest the wise world should look into your moan
　　And mock you with me after I am gone.
Sonnet 71

Beauty liv'd and died as flowers do now
Sonnet 68

After my death, -- dear love, forget me quite,
For you in me can nothing worthy prove;
Unless you would devise some virtuous lie,
To do more for me than mine own desert,
And hang more praise upon deceased I
Than niggard truth would willingly impart,
Sonnet 72

So are you to my thoughts as food to life
Sonnet 76

The earth can yield me but a common grave,
When you entombed in men's eyes shall lie
Sonnet 81

I never saw that you did painting need
And therefore to your fair no painting set;
I found, or thought I found, you did exceed
The barren tender of a poet's debt;
Sonnet 83

Such is my love, to thee I so belong,
That for thy right myself will bear all wrong.
Sonnet 88

O, what a happy title do I find,
Happy to have thy love, happy to die.
Sonnet 92

They that have power to hurt and will do none,
That do not do the thing they most do show,
Who, moving others, are themselves as stone,
Unmoved, cold, and to temptation slow;
They rightly do inherit heaven's graces
And husband nature's riches from expense;
They are the lords and owners of their faces,
Others but stewards of their excellence.
The summer's flower is to the summer sweet,
Though to itself it only live and die,
But if that flower with base infection meet,
The basest weed out-braves his dignity;
   For sweetest things turn sourest by their deeds;
   Lilies that fester smell far worse than weeds.
Sonnet 94

Let me not to the marriage of true minds
Admit impediments. Love is not love
Which alters when it alteration finds,
Or bends with the remover to remove:
O no; it is an ever-fixed mark,
That looks on tempests, and is never shaken;
It is the star to every wandering bark,

Whose worth's unknown, although his height be taken.
Love's not Time's fool, though rosy lips and cheeks
Within his bending sickle's compass come;
Love alters not with his brief hours and weeks,
But bears it out even to the edge of doom.
  If this be error and upon me proved,
  I never writ, nor no man ever loved.
Sonnet 116

My mistress' eyes are nothing like the sun;
Coral is far more red than her lips' red;
If snow be white, why then her breasts are dun;
If hairs be wires, black wires grow on her head.
I have seen roses damask'd, red and white,
But no such roses see I in her cheeks;
And in some perfumes is there more delight
Than in the breath that from my mistress reeks.
I love to hear her speak, yet well I know
That music hath a far more pleasing sound;
I grant I never saw a goddess go;
My mistress, when she walks, treads on the ground:
   And yet, by heaven, I think my love as rare
   As any she belied with false compare.
Sonnet 130

When my love swears that she is made of truth
I do believe her, though I know she lies,
That she might think me some untutor'd youth,
Unlearned in the world's false subtleties.
Thus vainly thinking that she thinks me young,
Although she knows my days are past the best,
Simply I credit her false speaking tongue:
On both sides thus is simple truth suppress'd.
But wherefore says she not she is unjust?
And wherefore say not I that I am old?
O, love's best habit is in seeming trust,
And age in love loves not to have years told:
   Therefore I lie with her and she with me,

And in our faults by lies we flatter'd be.
Sonnet 138

In faith, I do not love thee with mine eyes,
For they in thee a thousand errors note;
But 'tis my heart that loves what they despise,
Who in despite of view is pleased to dote;
Nor are mine ears with thy tongue's tune delighted,
Nor tender feeling, to base touches prone,
Nor taste, nor smell, desire to be invited
To any sensual feast with thee alone:
But my five wits nor my five senses can
Dissuade one foolish heart from serving thee,
Who leaves unsway'd the likeness of a man,
Thy proud hearts slave and vassal wretch to be:
   Only my plague thus far I count my gain,
   That she that makes me sin awards me pain.
Sonnet 141

The hardest knife ill-used doth lose his edge.
Sonnet 95

For I have sworn thee fair and thought thee bright,
Who art as black as hell, as dark as night.
Sonnet 147

VENUS AND ADONIS

Venus and Adonis is Shakespeare's first published work. The narrative poem tells of Venus, goddess of love, attempting to court Adonis, the handsomest man ever to exist. In an archetypical tale repeated even today, Adonis refuses to commit to her because he has a prior commitment…. to go hunting with his buddies.

Yes, the poem is the timeless tale of a woman whose love is more interested in hunting/fishing/sports/video games/cars/gambling/his career than he is in her…. with a hefty dose of tragedy added to it. It is also a tale of love vs lust, peppered with proverbs and insights into simplified, universal relationships and their woes.

The outcome of their encounter, if Venus had her way, would probably be the same as Meatloaf's *Paradise by the Dashboard Lights,* given Adonis' personality. Instead, Adonis has his way, goes hunting, and we get a version of *Billy, Don't be a Hero* as sung by Paper Lace. All of those are worth enjoying at least once, but if you can't be bothered reading all of Venus and Adonis (after listening to those two songs, of course) here are the best lines from the poem.

She red and hot as coals of glowing fire
He red for shame, but frosty in desire.
35-36

Backward she push'd him, as she would be thrust,
And govern'd him in strength, though not in lust.
42

Rain added to a river that is rank
Perforce will force it overflow the bank
71-72

Which long have rain'd, making her cheeks all wet;
And one sweet kiss shall pay this countless debt.
83-84

Make use of time, let not advantage slip;
Beauty within itself should not be wasted:
Fair flowers that are not gather'd in their prime
Rot and consume themselves in little time.
129-132

'Torches are made to light, jewels to wear,
Dainties to taste, fresh beauty for the use,
Herbs for their smell, and sappy plants to bear;
Things growing to themselves are growth's abuse:
Seeds spring from seeds, and beauty breedeth beauty;
Thou wast begot; to get it is thy duty.
163-168

O! had thy mother borne so hard a mind,
She had not brought forth thee, but died unkind.
203-204

'Pity,' she cries; 'some favour, some remorse!'
Away he springs, and hasteth to his horse.
258

O! what a war of looks was then between them;
Her eyes petitioners to his eyes suing;
His eyes saw her eyes as they had not seen them;
Her eyes woo'd still, his eyes disdain'd the wooing:
And all this dumb play had his acts made plain
With tears, which, chorus-like, her eyes did rain.

Full gently now she takes him by the hand,
A lily prison'd in a gaol of snow,
Or ivory in an alabaster band;
So white a friend engirts so white a foe:
This beauteous combat, wilful and unwilling,
Show'd like two silver doves that sit a-billing.
355-366

'Give me my hand,' saith he, 'why dost thou feel it?'
'Give me my heart,' saith she, 'and thou shalt have it;
O! give it me, lest thy hard heart do steel it,
And being steel'd, soft sighs can never grave it:
Then love's deep groans I never shall regard,
Because Adonis' heart hath made mine hard.'
373-378.

The sea hath bounds, but deep desire hath none
389

Who is so faint, that dare not be so bold
To touch the fire, the weather being cold?
401-402

'Had I no eyes but ears, my ears would love
That inward beauty and invisible;
Or were I deaf, thy outward parts would move

Each part in me that were but sensible:
Though neither eyes nor ears, to hear nor see,
Yet should I be in love by touching thee.

'Say, that the sense of feeling were bereft me,
And that I could not see, nor hear, nor touch,
And nothing but the very smell were left me,
Yet would my love to thee be still as much;
For from the stillitory of thy face excelling
Comes breath perfum'd that breedeth love by smelling.

'But O! what banquet wert thou to the taste,
Being nurse and feeder of the other four;
Would they not wish the feast might ever last,
And bid Suspicion double-lock the door,
Lest Jealousy, that sour unwelcome guest,
Should, by his stealing in, disturb the feast?'
433-450

For looks kill love, and love by looks reviveth
464

Were beauty under twenty locks kept fast,
Yet love breaks through and picks them all at last.
575-576

Her pleading hath deserv'd a greater fee;
She's Love, she loves, and yet she is not lov'd.
'Fie, fie!' he says, 'you crush me; let me go;
You have no reason to withhold me so.'
609-612

For misery is trodden on by many,
And being low never reliev'd by any
707-708

'In night,' quoth she, 'desire sees best of all.'
720

Be prodigal: the lamp that burns by night
Dries up his oil to lend the world his light
755-756

But gold that's put to use more gold begets.'
768

For know, my heart stands armed in mine ear,
And will not let a false sound enter there;
779-780

'Love comforteth like sunshine after rain,
But Lust's effect is tempest after sun;
Love's gentle spring doth always fresh remain,
Lust's winter comes ere summer half be done.
Love surfeits not, Lust like a glutton dies;
Love is all truth, Lust full of forged lies.
799-804

But like a stormy day, now wind, now rain,
Sighs dry her cheeks, tears make them wet again.
965-966

No flower was nigh, no grass, herb, leaf, or weed
But stole his blood and seem'd with him to bleed.
1054-1055

She lifts the coffer-lids that close his eyes,
Where, lo! two lamps, burnt out, in darkness lies;
1127-1128

She bows her head, the new-sprung flower to smell,
Comparing it to her Adonis' breath;
And says within her bosom it shall dwell,
Since he himself is reft from her by death:
1171-1174

THE GREAT BIG BOOK OF SHAKESPEARE QUOTES

THE RAPE OF LUCRECE

This is a beautifully crafted, powerful poem. While it was popular in its day, it is hard to enjoy today because the beautiful language describes something entirely terrible- a rape and the accompanying guilt of the victim. Additionally off-putting is the resolution to the rape and guilt; to say more would spoil the story. Here are the lines that best reach beyond the narrative of the text; for powerful tragic ballads, few come close to The Rape of Lucrece.

Beauty itself doth of itself persuade
The eyes of men without an orator;
30

Unstain'd thoughts do seldom dream on evil;
87

'O, what excuse can my invention make,
When thou shalt charge me with so black a deed?
225-226

All orators are dumb when beauty pleadeth;
268

As if the heavens should countenance his sin.
343

While she, the picture of pure piety,
Like a white hind under the gripe's sharp claws,
Pleads, in a wilderness where are no laws,
To the rough beast that knows no gentle right,

Nor aught obeys but his foul appetite
540

'Unruly blasts wait on the tender spring;
Unwholesome weeds take root with precious flowers;
The adder hisses where the sweet birds sing;
What virtue breeds iniquity devours
870

'O Time, thou tutor both to good and bad,
Teach me to curse him that thou taught'st this ill!
997-998

Though men can cover crimes with bold stern looks,
Poor women's faces are their own fault's books
1252-1253

To see sad sights moves more than hear them told;
For then eye interprets to the ear
The heavy motion that it doth behold,
When every part a part of woe doth bear.
'Tis but a part of sorrow that we hear:
Deep sounds make lesser noise than shallow fords,
And sorrow ebbs, being blown with wind of words.
1324-1330

And both she thinks too long with her remaining:
Short time seems long in ho's sharp sustaining:
Though woe be heavy, yet it seldom sleeps,
And they that watch see time how slow it creeps
1572-1575

QUOTES BY CATEGORY

Whether you are searching for understanding or a brilliant line for a speech, essay, or marriage proposal, this set of quotes by category will serve you well. Hopefully they whet your appetite to dive further into the source plays and poems.

If not, hopefully you still enjoy them.

THE GREAT BIG BOOK OF SHAKESPEARE QUOTES

AMBITION

Present fears are less than horrible imaginings.
Macbeth; 1.3.137-138.

Screw your courage to the sticking place and we'll not fail.
Macbeth; 1.7.60-61.

Why, then the worlds my oyster. Which I with sword will open.
The Merry Wives of Windsor; 2.2.4-5.

The gods themselves,
Humbling their deities to love, have taken
The shapes of beasts upon them.
The Winter's Tale; 4.4.25-27.

Ill weaved ambition, how much art thou shrunk.
Henry the IV Part 1: 5.4.88.

Go forward, and be chok'd with thy ambition!
Henry V; 2.4.111.

ARROGANCE

But man, proud man, dress'd in a little brief authority, most ignorant of what he's most assur'd,s glass essence, like an angry ape, plays such fantastic tricks before high heaven as makes the angels weep; who, with our spleens, would laugh themselves mortal.
Measure for Measure; 2.3.117-123

Our virtues would be proud if our faults whipt them not; and our crimes would despair if they were not cherish'd by our virtues.
All's Well That Ends Well: 4.3.70-72.

You are not worth the dust which the rude wind
blows in your face.
King Lear- 4.2.30-31

You are the hare of whom the proverb goes,
whose valour plucks dead lions by the beard.
King John; 2.1.137-138.

Respect, which the proud soul never pays but to the proud.
Henry I part 1; 1.3.9.

Small things make base men proud.
4.1.106.

ATTITUDE

What should a man do but be merry?
Hamlet 3.2.101.

Know thou this, that men are as the time is;
to be tender-minded does not become a sword.
King Lear; 5.3.31-33

If we should fail… we fail, but screw your courage to the sticking-place, and we'll not fail.
Macbeth; 1.7.58-60.

Against ill chances men are ever merry;
But heaviness foreruns the good event.
Henry the IV part 2: 4.2.81-82.

The tiger will be mild whiles she doth mourn.
Henry the VI part 3; 3.1.39.

I should be as merry as the day is long.
King John; 4.1.18.

BEAUTY

Beauty proveth thieves sooner than gold.
As You Like It; 1.3.106.

Honesty coupled to beauty is to have a sauce to sugar.
As You Like It; 3.3.27.

For where is any author in the world
Teaches such beauty as a woman's eye?
Love's Labour Lost; 4.3.308-309.

The weakest kind of fruit drops earliest to the ground.
The Merchant of Venice; 4.1.115.

Her beauty and her brain go not together.
Cymbeline; 1.2.28.

Beauty itself doth of itself persuade
The eyes of men without an orator;
The Rape of Lucrece; 30

How with this rage shall beauty hold a plea,
Whose action is no stronger than a flower?
Sonnet 65

Beauty liv'd and died as flowers do now
Sonnet 68

'Tis beauty that doth oft make women proud
Henry the VI part 3; 1.4.128.

BUSINESS

A good wit will make use of anything. I will turn diseases to commodity.
Henry the IV part 2: 1.2.231-232.

I am right loath to go;
There is some ill a-brewing towards my rest,
for I did dream of money-bags tonight.
The Merchant of Venice; 2.5.16-18.

Not I, but my affairs, have made you wait.
The Merchant of Venice; 2.6.21.

All that glisters is not gold.
The Merchant of Venice; 2.7.66.

If it were done when 'tis done, then 'twere well it were done quickly.
1.7.1-2.

Your cares set up do not pluck my cares down.
Richard II; 4.1.195.

All things that are with more spirit chased than enjoyed.
2.6.12-13.

Is not the truth the truth?
Henry the IV part 1; 2.4.224.

Truth loves open dealing.
Henry the VIII;3.1.39.

BRAVERY, COURAGE AND CAUTION

The better part of valour is discretion.
Henry the IV part 1; 5.4.119.

Wisely and slow. They stumble that run fast.
Romeo and Juliet; 2.3.94.

You have too much respect upon the world; they lose it that do buy it with much care.
The Merchant of Venice; 1.1.74-75.

Things done well and with a care exempt themselves from fear.
Henry the VIII; 1.2.88-89.

Let not our babbling dreams affright our souls.
Conscience is but a word that cowards use,
Devised at first to keep the strong in awe.
Our strong arms be our conscience, swords our law.
March on. Join bravely. Let us to it pell mell,
If not to heaven, then hand in hand to hell.
Richard III: 5.3.309-314.

Out of this nettle, danger, we pluck the flower, safety.
Henry the IV part 1; 2.3.6-7.

CURSES AND INSULTS

He's a devil, a devil, a very fiend.
Why, she's a devil, a devil, the devil's dam.
The Taming of the Shrew; 3.2.151-152.

You are a fool.
Twelfth Night; 1.3.83.

We took him for a coward, but he's the very devil incarnate.
Twelfth Night; 5.1.172-173.

I think he be transform'd into a beast;
for I can nowhere find him like a man.
As You Like It; 2.7.1-2.

O that ever I was born!
The Winter's Tale; 4.1.57.

Let vultures gripe thy guts!
The Merry Wives of Windsor: 1.3.82.

I thank them; and would send them back the plague
Could I but catch it for them.
Timon of Athens; 5.1.135-136.

I will beat thee into handsomeness.
Troilus and Cressida;2.1.13-14.

You whoreson cur!
Troilus and Cressida;2.1.39.

Thou stool for a witch!
Troilus and Cressida;2.1.41.

You scurvy villain ass!
Troilus and Cressida; 2.1.44.

A pox damn you, you muddy rascal!
Henry the IV Part 2; 2.4.39-40.

Hang yourself, you muddy conger, hang yourself.
Henry the IV Part 2; 2.4.51-52.

You two never meet but you fall to some discord.
Henry the IV Part 2; 2.3.52-53.

What! You poor, base, rascally, cheating, lack-linen mate!
Henry the IV Part 2; 2.3.115-116.

You filthy bung, away!
Henry the IV Part 2; 2.3.120.

Thou wast born to be a plague to men.
Henry the VI Part 3: 5.5.28.

Blush, blush, thou lump of foul deformity.
Richard III: 1.2.57.

Cancel his bond of life, dear God, I pray,
That I may live and say, "The dog is dead".
Richard III: 4.4.77-78.

Thou cam'st on earth to make the earth my hell.
Richard III: 4.4.166.

EDUCATION AND LEARNING

Thou hast
most traitorously corrupted the youth of the realm
in erecting a grammar school; and whereas,
before, our forefathers had no other books but the
score and the tally, thou hast caused printing to be
used, and, contrary to the King his crown and dignity,
thou hast built a paper mill. It will be proved
to thy face that thou hast men about thee that usually
talk of a noun and a verb and such abominable
words as no Christian ear can endure to hear.
Thou hast appointed justices of peace to call poor
men before them about matters they were not able
to answer. Moreover, thou hast put them in prison;
and, because they could not read, thou hast
hanged them, when indeed only for that cause
they have been most worthy to live.
Henry the VI Part 2: 4.7.31-43.

I'll not be tied to hours nor pointed times,
But learn my lessons as I please myself.
The Taming of the Shrew: 3.1.19-20.

ETHICS AND VILLAINY

It is great sin to swear unto a sin,
But greater sin to keep a sinful oath.
Who can be bound by any solemn vow
To do a murd'rous deed, to rob a man,
To force a spotless virgin's chastity,
To reave the orphan of his patrimony,
To wring the widow from her customed right,
And have no other reason for this wrong
But that he was bound by a solemn oath?
Henry VI Part 2: 5.1.182-190.

But for a kingdom any oath may be broken.
I would break a thousand oaths to rein one year.
Hery the VI Part 3: 1.2.15-16.

Though I wish thy death,
I will not be thy executioner.
Richard III: 1.2.184-185.

FRIENDS AND FRIENDSHIP

I leave myself, my friends, and all for love.
Two Gentlemen of Verona; 1.1.65

'Twixt such friends as we few words suffice.
The Taming of the Shrew; 1.2.63-64.

My friends were poor, but honest; so's my love.
All's Well that Ends Well; 1.3.186.

The better for my foes and the worse for my friends.
Twelfth Night; 5.1.10.

Those friends thou hast, and heir adoption tried,
Grapple them to thy soul with hoops of steel
Hamlet; 1.3.62-63.

What need we have any friends if we should ne'er have need of em?
Timon of Athens; 1.2.90.

O, let not virtue seek
remuneration for the thing it was;
for beauty, wit, high birth, vigour of bone, desert in service, love,
friendship, charity, are subjects all
to envious and calumniating time.
Troilus and Cressida; 3.3.169-174.

I count myself in nothing else so happy
as in a sold rememb'ring my good friends.
Richard II; 2.3.46-47.

Blessed are they that have been my friends
Henry IV part 2; 5.3.136.

There is flattery in friendship
Henry V; 3.7.113.

How much thou wrong'st me, heaven be my judge.
Die, damned wretch, the curse of her that bare thee!
Henry VI Part 2:4.10.75-76.

We were but hollow friends.
Henry VI Part 2; 3.2.66.

GIVING

Men take women's gifts for impudence.
Pericles, Prince of Tyre; 2.3.70.

O you gods!
why do you make us love your goodly gifts,
and snatch them straight away?
Pericles, Prince of Tyre; 3.1.22-24.

Rich gifts wax poor when givers prove unkind.
Hamlet; 3.1.100-101.

I can no other answer make but thanks,
And thanks, and ever thanks.
Twelfth Night: 3.3.14-15.

I am fortune's steward.
Henry the IV part 1; 5.1.129.

FAME AND FATE

When no friends are by, men praise themselves.
Titus Andronicus; 5.3.118.

There's hope a good man's name will outlive his life half a year.
Hamlet; 3.2.135-137.

I am constant to my purposes.
Hamlet; 5.2.193.

Not a whit, we defy augury: there's a special
providence in the fall of a sparrow. If it be now,
'tis not to come; if it be not to come, it will be
now; if it be not now, yet it will come: the
readiness is all: since no man has aught of what he
leaves, what is't to leave betimes? Let be.
Hamlet; 5.2.208-210.

Let life be short, else shame will be too long.
Henry V; 4.4.23.

GRIEVING AND SORROW

One sorrow never comes but brings an heir
that may succeed as his inheritor.
Pericles, Prince of Tyre; 1.4.63-64.

Weigh our sorrow with our comfort
The Tempest; 2.1.9-10

When sorrows come, they come not single spies,
but in battalions!
Hamlet; 4.5.75-76.

Could we but learn from whence his sorrows grow, we would as willingly give cure as we know.
Romeo and Juliet; 1.1.152-153

Sad hours seem long
Romeo and Juliet; 1.1.161

Parting is such sweet sorrow,
Romeo and Juliet; 2. 1. 185.

Sorrow concealed, like an oven stopp'd,
doth burn the heart to cinders where it is.
Titus Andronicus; 2.4.36-37.

I will instruct my sorrows to be proud,
for grief is proud, and makes his owner stoop.
King John; 3.1.68-69.

My grief's so great,
that no supporter but the huge firm earth can hold it up.
King John; 3.1.71-72

To see sad sights moves more than hear them told;
For then eye interprets to the ear
The heavy motion that it doth behold,
When every part a part of woe doth bear.

'Tis but a part of sorrow that we hear:
Deep sounds make lesser noise than shallow fords,
And sorrow ebbs, being blown with wind of words.
The Rape of Lucrece; 1324-1330

HONESTY

There's no art to find the mind's construction in the face.
Macbeth: 1.4.11-13.

Let not light see my black and deep desires.
Macbeth: 1.4.51.

False face must hide what the false heart doth know.
Macbeth: 1.7.82.

There are liars and swearers enow to beat the honest men and hang them up.
Macbeth; 4.2.53-55.

When love begins to sicken and decay,
it useth an enforced ceremony.
Julius Caesar; 4.1.20-21.

I am arm'd so strong in honesty
That they pass by me as the idle wind,
Which I respect not.
Julius Caesar; 4.3.67-69.

There's no trust, no faith, no honesty in men
Romeo and Juliet; 3.2.85-86.

I never was nor never will be false.
Richard III: 4.4.495.

HONOR AND INTEGRITY

Herein you war against your reputation.
The Comedy of Errors:3.1.86.

We to ourselves prove false.
Love's Labours Lost; 5.2.760.

As waggish boys in game themselves forswear,
So the boy love is perjur'd everywhere.
A Midsummer Night's Dream: 1.1.240-241.

Kindness in women, not their beauteous looks, shall win my love.
The Taming of the Shrew; 4.2.40-41.

Though authority be a stubborn bear, yet it is oft led by the nose with gold.
The Winter's Tale; 4.4.789-790.

Mine honour is my life; both grow in one;
Take honour from me and my life is done.
Richard II; 1.1.182-183.

HOME

Home keeping youths have ever homely wits.
1.1.2.
The Two Gentlemen of Verona

When I was at home, I was in a better place;
but travelers must be content.
As You Like It; 2.4.12-13.

This castle hath a pleasing seat; the air nimbly and sweetly recommends itself unto our gentle senses.
Macbeth; 1.6.1-3.

I would give all my fame for a pot of ale and safety.
Henry V; 3.2.11.

HOPE

Oft expectations fails, and most oft there
where most it promises; and oft it hits
where hope is coldest, and despair fits most.
All's Well that End's Well; 2.1.141-143.

You must take your chance.
The Merchant of Venice; 2.1.38.

Things without all remedy should be without regard; what's done is done.
Macbeth; 3.2.10-12

From the dejected state wherein he is,
he hopes by you his fortunes yet may flourish.
Pericles, Prince of Tyre; 2.2.46-47.

How shalt thou hope for mercy, rendering none?
The Merchant of Venice; 4.1.88.

Hope is a lover's staff.
The Two Gentlemen of Verona; 3.1.245.

God shall be my hope,
my stay, my guide, and lantern to my feet.
Henry the VI part 2; 2.3.23-24.

INDISCRETION

Can one desire too much of a good thing?
As You Like It; 4.1.107.

Our indiscretion sometimes serves us well, when our deep lots do pall; and that should learn us there's a divinity that shapes our ends, rough-hew them how we will.
Hamlet; 5.2.8-11.

We will solicit heaven and move the gods
to send down Justice for to wreak our wrongs.
Titus Andronicus; 4.3.49-50.

I would my means were greater and my waist slenderer. Henry the IV part 1; 1.2.134-135.

But when the fox hath once got in his nose,
He'll soon find means to make the body follow.
Henry the VI Part 3: 4.7.25-26.

JUDGMENT AND JUSTICE

Sufficieth, my reasons are both good and weighty.
The Taming of the Shrew;1.1.241

Defect of judgment is oft the cease of fear.
Cymbeline; 4.2.112-113.

Virtue itself scapes not calumnious strokes.
Hamlet; 1.3.38.

Use every man after his desert, and who shall scape the whipping?
Hamlet; 2.2.522-523.

Did not great Julius bleeed for justice sake?
What villain touch'd his body, that did stab,
And not for justice?
Julius Caesar; 4.3.19-21.

The world is not thy friend, nor the world's law;
the world affords no law to make thee rich;
then be not poor, but break it and take this.
Romeo and Juliet; 5.1.72-74.

When law can do no right,
let it be lawful that law bar no wrong.
King John; 3.1.185-186.

God defend the right.
Henry the VI part 2; 2.3.55.

KILLING AND DEATH

All deaths are too few, the sharpest too easy.
The Winter's Tale; 4.4.769.

The stroke of death is as a lover's pinch,
which hurts and is desir'd.
Troilus and Cressida; 5.2.292-293.

If any think brave death outweighs bad life
and that his country's dearer than himself,
let him alone.
Coriolanus; 1.6.71-72.

Who would these fardels bear,
to grunt and sweat under a weary life,
but that the dread of something after death—
the undiscover'd country, from whose bourn
no traveller returns-- puzzles the will,
and makes us rather bear those ills we have
than fly to others that we know not of?
Thus conscience does make cowards of us all.
Hamlet; 3.1.76-83.

Love lead fortune or else fortune love.
Hamlet; 3.2.198.

He that is not guilty of his own death shortens not his own life.
Hamlet; 5.1.20.

It is silliness to live when to live is torment; and then have we a prescription to die when death is our physician.
Othello; 1.3.308-309.

Death lies upon her like an untimely frost
Upon the sweetest flower of all the field.
Romeo and Juliet; 4.5.28-29.

How oft when men are at the point of death have they been

merry!
Romeo and Juliet; 5.1.88-89.

'Tis strange that death should sing.
King John; 5.7.20.

Though death be poor, it ends a mortal woe.
Richard II; 3.1.152.

Thou owest god a death.
Henry IV part 1; 5.1.126.

Death, as the psalmist saith, is certain to all; all shall die.
Henry the IV part 2; 3.2.33.

So bad a death argues a monstrous life.
Henry the VI part 2; 3.3.30.

Falstaff: What, is the old king dead?
Pistol: As nail in door.
Henry the IV part 2; 5.3.119-120.

From forth the kennel of thy wound hath crept
A hell-hound that doth hunt us all to death.
Richard III; 4.4.47-48.

After my death, -- dear love, forget me quite,
For you in me can nothing worthy prove;
Sonnet 72.

LANGUAGE, WORDS, AND COMMUNICATION

Thou wouldst as soon go kindle fire with snow
as seek to quench the fire of love with words.
Two Gentlemen of Verona; 2.7.19-20

Dumb jewels in often in their silent kind
more than quick words do move a woman's mind.
Two Gentlemen of Verona; 3.1.91-92

They that dally nicely with words may quickly make them wanton.
Twelfth Night; 3.1.13.

Fair payment for foul words is more than due.
Love's Labour Lost; 4.1.19.

Honest plain words best pierce the ear of grief.
Love's Labour Lost; 5.2.741.

You cram these words into my ears against the stomach of my sense.
The Tempest; 2.1.99-100

You taught me language, and my profit on't is, I know how to curse. The red plague rid you for learning me your language.
The Tempest; 1.2.425-428

Words without thoughts never to heaven go.
Hamlet; 3.3.98.

He has strangled his language in his tears.
Henry the VIII; 5.1.157.

Words, words, words.
Hamlet; 2.2.191.

Words, words, mere words, no matter from the heart.

Troilus and Cressida; 5.3.108.

These words are razors to my wounded heart.
Titus Andronicus; 1.1.314.

I was never so bethum'p with words!
King John; 2.1.466.

LOVE AND LUST

The course of true love never did run smooth.
A Midsummer Night's Dream; 1.1.136

My heart unto yours I knit.
A Midsummer Night's Dream; 2.2.48.

And yet, to say the truth, reason and love keep little company together now-a-days.
A Midsummer Night's Dream; 3.1.133-134.

I leave myself, my friends, and all for love.
Two Gentlemen of Verona; 1.1.65

They do not love that do not show their love.
O, they love least that let men know their love.
Two Gentlemen of Verona; 1.2.31-32

Yet writers say, as in the sweetest bud the eating canker dwells, so eating love inhabits the finest wits of all.
Two Gentlemen of Verona;1.1.42-43

Love is blind.
Two Gentlemen of Verona; 2.1.63

Parting strikes poor lovers dumb.
Two Gentlemen of Verona; 2.2.21

Love's a mighty lord,
and hath so humbled me as I confess
there is no woe to his correction
nor to his service no such joy on earth.
Two Gentlemen of Verona; 2.4.132-135

For love, thou knowest, is full of jealousy.
Two Gentlemen of Verona; 2.4.173

Thou wouldst as soon go kindle fire with snow

as seek to quench the fire of love with words.
Two Gentlemen of Verona; 2.7.19-20

Hope is a lover's staff.
Two Gentlemen of Verona; 3.1.245.

Alas, how love can trifle with itself!
Two Gentlemen of Verona; 4.4.179

love will not be spurred to what it loathes.
Two Gentlemen of Verona; 5.1.7

I pray, sir, tell me, is it possible
that love should of a sudden take such hold?
The Taming of the Shrew; 1.1.142-142.

I had rather hear my dog bark at a crow than rather hear a man swear that he loves me.
Much Ado About Nothing; 1.1.111-112.

A man loves the meat in his youth that he cannot endure in his age.
Much Ado About Nothing; 2.3.218-219.

I do love nothing in the world so well as you. Is not that strange?
Much Ado About Nothing; 4.1.266-267.

Shall love, in building, grow so ruinous?
The Comedy of Errors; 3.2.6.

Love like a shadow flies when shadow love pursues;
pursuing that that flies, and flying what pursues.
The Merry Wives of Windsor; 2.2.187-188

My friends were poor, but honest; so's my love.
All's Well that End's Well; 1.3.186.

If music be the food of love, play on.
Twelfth Night; 1.1.1.

Love sought is good but given unsought is better.
Twelfth Night; 3.1.152.

We that are true lovers run into strange capers;
but as all is mortal in nature, so is all nature in love mortal in filly.
As You Like It; 2.4.50-52.

Love is merely a madness; and I tell you, deserves as well a dark house and a whip as madmen do and the reason why they are not so punish'd and cured is that the lunacy is so ordinary that the whippers are in love too. Yet I profess curing it by counsel.
As You Like It; 3.2.367-372.

Love is merely a madness; and I tell you, deserves as well a dark house and a whip as madmen do and the reason why they are not so punish'd and cured is that the lunacy is so ordinary that the whippers are in love too. Yet I profess curing it by counsel.
As You Like It; 3.2.367-372.

Love is a devil. There is not evil angel but love.
Love's Labour Lost; 1.2.162-163.

There is not half a kiss to choose who loves another best.
The Winter's Tale; 4.4.175-176.

O you gods!
Why do you make us love your goodly gifts,
and snatch them straight away?
Pericles, Prince of Tyre; 3.1.22-24.

O, you beast!
O faithless coward! O dishonest wretch!
Wilt thou be made a man out of my vice?
3.1.137-139.

Love talks with better knowledge and knowledge with dearer love.
Measure for Measure: 3.2.140.

If I love mine honour,
I lose myself.
Anthony and Cleopatra; 3.4.22-23.

Doubt thou the stars are fire;
Doubt that the sun doth move;

Doubt truth to be a liar;
But never doubt I love.
Hamlet; 2.2.115-118.

Is love a tender thing? It is too rough,
too rude, too boist'rous , and it pricks like thorn.
Romeo and Juliet; 1.4.25-26

If love be rough with you, be rough with love.
Romeo and Juliet; 1.4.27

Did my heart love till now? Forswear it, sight!
Romeo and Juliet; 1.5.52

My only love sprung from my only hate!
Romeo and Juliet; 1.5.139

Can I go forward when my heart is here?
Romeo and Juliet; 2.1.1.

If love be blind, love cannot hit the mark.
Romeo and Juliet; 2.1.33.

This bud of love, by summer's ripening breath,
May prove a beauteous flow'r when next we meet.
Romeo and Juliet; 2.2.121-123.

Love goes toward love as schoolboys from their books;
But love from love, toward school with heavy looks.
Romeo and Juliet; 2.2.157-158.

Young men's love then lies
Not truly in their hearts, but in their eyes.
Romeo and Juliet; 2.3.68-69.
These violent delights have violent ends
And in their triumph die, like fire and powder,
Which, as they kiss, consumer. The sweetest honey is loathsome
in his onw deliciousness
And in the taste confounds the appetite.
Therefore, love moderately; long love doth so'
Too swift arrives as tardy as too slow.
Romeo and Juliet; 2.6.9-15.

The love I bear thee can afford no better terms than this; thou are at villain.
Romeo and Juliet; 3.1.59-60.

No, 'tis not so deep as a well, nor so wide as a church door; but tis enough, 'twill serve. As for me tomorrow, and you shall find me a grave man.
Romeo and Juliet; 3.1.93-97.

O, I am fortune's fool!
Romeo and Juliet; 3.1.134.

If love be blind, it best agrees with night.
Romeo and Juliet; 3.2.9-10.

Love give me strength!
Romeo and Juliet; 4.1.125.

Yet hasty marriage seldom proveth well.
Henry the VI part 3: 4.1.18.

Do not kill
the spirit of love with a perpetual dullness.
Sonnet 56

So true a fool is love that in your will,
though you do any thing, he thinks no ill.
Sonnet 57

After my death, -- dear love, forget me quite,
For you in me can nothing worthy prove;
Sonnet 72

Such is my love, to thee I so belong,
That for thy right myself will bear all wrong.
Sonnet 88

O, what a happy title do I find,
Happy to have thy love, happy to die.
Sonnet 92

The entirety of Sonnets 116, 130, 138, and 141.

MEN AND WOMEN

It is the lesser blot, modesty finds,
Women to change their shapes than men their minds.
Two Gentlemen of Verona; 5.4.108-109

To be slow in words is a woman's only virtue.
3.1.33-336.

A woman mov'd is like a fountain troubled.
The Taming of the Shrew; 55.2.142.

I am asham'd that women are so simple to offer war where they should kneel for peace.
The Taming of the Shrew; 55.2.161-162.

We men may say more, swear more, but indeed
Our shows are more than will; for still we prove
Much in our vows, but little in our love.
Twelfth Night; 2.4.114-116.

The more pity that fools may not speak wisely what wise men do foolishly.
As You Like It; 1.2.78.

I thank god I am not a woman, to be touch'd with so many giddy offences as he hath generally tax'd their whole sex withal.
As You Like It; 3.2.325-326.

I think he be transform'd into a beast;
for I can nowhere find him like a man.
As You Like It; 2.7.1-2.

There's many a man hath more hair than wit
The Taming of the Shrew; 2.2.81

We are gentlemen

that neither in our hearts nor outward eyes
envy the great nor shall the low despise.
Pericles, Prince of Tyre; 2.3.24-26.

Well, if fortune be a woman, she's a good wench this year.
The Merchant of Venice; 2.2.152.

Some rise by sin, and some by virtue fall.
Measure for Measure; 2.1.37

A man loves the meat in his youth that he cannot endure in his age.
Much Ado About Nothing; 2.3.218-219.

We men may say more, swear more, but indeed
Our shows are more than will; for still we prove
Much in our vows, but little in our love.
Twelfth Night; 2.4.114-116.

Faith, there have been many great men that have flatter'd the people, who ne'er loved them.
Coriolanus; 2.2.7-8.

Would we had all such wives, that the men might go to wars with the women!
Anthony and Cleopatra; 2.2.69-70.

All men's faces are true, whatsoe'er their hands are but there is never a fair woman that has a true face.
Anthony and Cleopatra; 2.6.97-98.

O, my fortunes have corrupted honest men!
Anthony and Cleopatra; 4.5.16-17.

Wert thou a man
thou wouldst have mercy on me.
Anthony and Cleopatra; 5.2.173-174.

Faith, there have been many great men that have flatter'd the people, who ne'er loved them.
Coriolanus; 2.2.7-8.

What a piece of work is man!

Hamlet; 2.2.303-304.

Man delights not me-- no, nor woman neither, though by your smiling you seem to say so.
Hamlet; 2.2.308-309.

An old man is twice a child.
Hamlet; 2.2.380.

Know thou this, that men are as the time is;
to be tender-minded does not become a sword.
King Lear; 5.3.31-33.

I dare do all that becomes a man; he that will do more is none.
Macbeth; 1.7.46-47.

There are liars and swearers enow to beat the honest men and hang them up.
Macbeth; 4.2.53-55.

Dispute it like a man.
Macbeth; 4.3.218.

I shall do so; but I must also feel it like a man.
Macbeth; 4.3.190.

Men should be that they seem; or those that be not, would they might seem none!
Othello; 3.3.131-132.

Women may fall when there's no strength left in men.
Romeo and Juliet; 2.3.80.

I wonder men dare trust themselves with men.
Timon of Athens; 1.2.42.
Men's vows are women's traitors.
Cymbeline; 3.4.51-52.

Wounds heal ill that men do give themselves.
Troilus and Cressida; 3.3.229.

We worldly men
have miserable, mad, mistaking eyes.
Titus Andronicus; 5.2.66-67.

When no friends are by, men praise themselves.
Titus Andronicus; 5.3.118

More are men's ends marked than their lives before.
Richard II; 2.1.11.

'tis no sin for a man to labour in his vocation.
Henry the IV Part 1; 1.2.101

I am not only witty in myself, but the cause that wit is in other men.
Henry the IV part 2; 1.2.9-10.

Lord, Lord, how subject we old men are to this vice of lying.
Henry the IV part 2; 3.2.294-295

Women are shrews, both short and tall.
Henry the IV part 2; 5.3.32.

When a world of men
Could not prevail with all their oratory,
Yet hath a woman's kindness overrul'd.
Henry the VI part 1: 2.2.48-50.

A woman's general; what should we fear?
Henry the VI part 3; 1.2.68.

Women are soft, mild, pitiful, and flexible
Henry the VI part 3; 1.4.141.

Though men can cover crimes with bold stern looks,
Poor women's faces are their own fault's books
The Rape of Lucrece; 1252-1253

MONEY

Too little payment for so great a debt.
The Taming of the Shrew; 55.2.153.

All things that are with more spirit chased than enjoyed.
The Merchant of Venice; 2.6.12-13.

All that glisters is not gold.
The Merchant of Venice; 2.7.66.

To business that we love we rise betimes,
and go to't with delight.
Anthony and Cleopatra; 4.4.20-21.

Neither a borrower nor a lender be'
For loan oft loses both itself and friend,
and borrowing dulls the edge of husbandry.
Hamlet; 1.3.75-77.

Love lead fortune or else fortune love.
Hamlet; 3.2.198.

Commodity, the bias of the world
King John; 2.1.574.

A good wit will make use of anything; I shall turn diseases to commodity.
Henry IV Part 2;1.2.231-233.

NEWS

For slander lives upon succession
For ever hous'd where it gets possession.
The Comedy of Errors; 3.1.105-106

I that do bring the news made not the match.
Anthony and Cleopatra; 2.5.68.

Though it be honest, it is never good to bring bad news.
Anthony and Cleopatra; 2.5.85-86

My dreams presage some joyful news at hand.
Romeo and Juliet; 5.1.1-2.

Which of you will stop the vent of hearing when loud rumour speaks?
Henry the IV part 2; 1.1.1-2.

If Henry were recall'd to life again, this news would cause him once more to yield the ghost.
Henry the VI part 1; 1.1.65-66.

Fortune, that arrant whore, ne'er turns the key to th' poor.
King Lear; 2.4.51-52.

The weight of this sad time we must obey;
speak what we feel, not what we ought to say.
King Lear; 5.3.323-324.

OPINION

Old fashions please me best; I am not so nice
to change true rules for odd inventions.
The Taming of the Shrew.3.1.78-79.

Opinion's but a fool that makes us scan
the outward habit by the inward man
Pericles, Prince of Tyre; 2.2.56-57.

Seldom but that pity begets you a good opinion.
Pericles, Prince of Tyre; 4.2.121-122.

By heaven, it is as proper to our age
to cast beyond ourselves in our opinions
As it is common for the younger sort
to lack discretion.
Hamlet; 2.1.114-117.

What is a man, if his chief good and market of his time
be but to sleep and feed? A beast, no more.
Sure, he that made us with such large discourse,
looking before and after, gave us not
that capability and god-like reason
to fust in us unused.
Hamlet; 4.4.32-39.

A plague of opinion!
A man may wear it on both sides, like a leather jerkin.
Troilus and Cressida; 3.3.203-204.

PASSION

Men can counsel and speak comfort to that grief which they themselves not feel; but, tasting it, their counsel turns to passion, which before would give precipitable medicine to rage.
Much Ado About Nothing; 5.1.20-24.

It is the show and seal of nature's truth,
where love's strong passion is impress'd in youth.
All's Well That End's Well; 1.3.123-124.

Few love to hear the sins they love to act.
Pericles, Prince of Tyre; 1.1.92.

The passions of the mind,
that have their first conception by misdread,
have after-nourishment and life by care
Pericles, Prince of Tyre; 1.2.11-13.

Affection, mistress of passion, sways it to the mood of what it likes or loathes.
The Merchant of Venice; 4.1.50-52.

The lady doth protest too much, methinks.
Hamlet; 3.2.224.

Give me that man that is not passion's slave, and I will wear him in my heart's core, ay, in my heart of heart,
As I do thee.
Hamlet; 3.2.69-72

Of all base passions fear is most accurs'd.
Henry VI part 1; 5.2.18.

PEACE

What would you have, you curs,
that like not peace nor war?
Coriolanus; 1.1.167-168.

War... it exceeds peace as far as day does night.
Coriolanus; 4.5.221-222.

Better be with the dead, whom we, to gain our peace, have sent to peace than on the torture of the mind to live in restless ecstasy.
Macbeth; 3.2.18-21

Ah, what a life were this! how sweet! how lovely!
gives not the hawthorn-bush a sweeter shade
to shepherds looking on their silly sheep,
than doth a rich embroider'd canopy
to kings that fear their subjects' treachery?
O, yes, it doth; a thousand-fold it doth.
2.5.41-46.

In peace there's nothing so becomes a man
as modest stillness and humility;
Henry V; 3.1.3-4.

PLEASURE

Oft our pleasures, to ourselves unjust,
destroy our friends, and after weep their dust.
All's Well That End's Well; 5.3.63-64.

O, how bitter a thing it is to look into happiness through another man's eyes.
As You Like It; 5.1.39-40.

Here face the book of praises, where is read
nothing but curious pleasures
Pericles, Prince of Tyre; 1.1.14-15.

What our contempts doth often hurt from us we wish it ours again; the present pleasure, by revolution low'ring, does become the opposite of itself.
Anthony and Cleopatra; 1.2.120-123.

Give me a gash, put me to present pain,
lest this great sea of joys rushing upon me
o'erbear the shores of my mortality.
Pericles, Prince of Tyre; 5.1.189-191.

All things that are with more spirit chased than enjoyed.
The Merchant of Venice; 2.6.12-13.

Having such a blessing in his lady,
he finds the joys of heaven here on earth
The Merchant of Venice; 3.5.66-67.

O god, that men should put an enemy in their mouths to steal away their brains! That we should with joy, pleasance, revel and applause, transform ourselves into beasts!
Othello; 2.3.280-283.

REVENGE

Kindness, ever stronger than revenge.
As You Like It; 4.3.127.

How all occasions do inform against me, and spur my dull revenge!
Hamlet; 4.4.32.

Revenge should have no bounds.
Hamlet; 4.7.128.

Let's make medicine of our great revenge, to cure this deadly grief.
Macbeth; 4.3.14-17.

He's poor, and that's revenge enough.
Timon of Athens; 3.4.63.

To revenge is no valour, but to bear.
Timon of Athens; 3.5.39.

I'll be merry in my revenge.
Cymbeline; 3.5.145-146.

Tell him revenge is come to join with him,
and work confusion on his enemies
Titus Andronicus; 5.2.7-8.

Oft have I heard that grief softens the mind
and makes it fearful and degenerate;
Think therefore on revenge and cease to weep.
Henry the VI part 2; 4.4.1-3.

The smallest worm will turn, being trodden on.
And doves will peck in safeguard of their brood.
Henry the VI part 3; 2.2.17-18.

REASON

What is a man, if his chief good and market of his time
be but to sleep and feed? A beast, no more.
Sure, he that made us with such large discourse,
looking before and after, gave us not
that capability and god-like reason
to fust in us unused.
Hamlet; 4.4.32-39.

O, reason not the need! Our basest beggars
are in the poorest thing superfluous.
King Lear; 2.4.263-264.

Good reasons, must, of force, give place to better.
Julius Caesar; 4.3.201.

TRUTH

And yet, to say the truth, reason and love keep little company together now-a-days.
A Midsummer Night's Dream; 3.1.133-134

Look when I vow, I weep; and vows so born,
in their nativity all truth appears.
A Midsummer Night's Dream; 3.2.124-125.

There is scarce truth enough alive to make societies secure.
Measure for Measure; 3.1.211-212

Do not banish reason for inequality, but let your reason serve to make the truth appear where it seems hid and hide the false seems true.
Measure for Measure; 5.1.62-65

Though thou speak'st truth,
methinks thou speak'st not well.
Coriolanus; 1.6.13-14.

I will not do't,
lest I surcease to honour mine own truth,
and by my body's action teach my mind
a most inherent baseness.
Coriolanus; 3.2.120-123.

Let me have no lying; it becomes none but tradesmen.
Coriolanus; 4.4.712.

Doubt thou the stars are fire;
Doubt that the sun doth move;
Doubt truth to be a liar;
But never doubt I love.
Hamlet; 2.2.115-118.

I speak no more than truth

thou dost not speak so much.
Troilus and Cressida; 1.1.63-64.

By chance, not by truth.
King John; 1.1.169.

I can teach thee, coz, to shame the devil by telling truth.
Henry the VI part 1; 3.1.58-59.

Is not the truth the truth?
Henry IV part 1: 2.4.224.

Lord, Lord, how this world is given to lying!
Henry the IV part 1; 5.4.143.

Lord, Lord, how subject we old men are to this vice of lying.
Henry the IV part 2; 3.2.294-295.

God and good men hate so foul a liar.
Richard II; 1.1.114.

Truth loves open dealing.
Henry the VIII; 3.1.39.

UNDERSTANDING

'He that is giddy thinks the world turns around'
The Taming of the Shrew; 5.2.26.

When I do tell thee there my hopes lie drown'd,
reply not in how many fathoms deep
they lie indrench'd.
Troillus and Cressida; 1.1.47-49.

This blows my heart.
If swift thought break it not, a swifter mean
Shall outstrike thought; but thought will do't, I feel.
Anthony and Cleopatra; 4.6.34-36.

The weight of this sad time we must obey;
speak what we feel, not what we ought to say.
King Lear; 5.3.323-324.

Dispute it like a man.
Macbeth; 4.3.218.

I shall do so; but I must also feel it like a man.
Macbeth; 4.3.190.

Thou canst not speak of that thou dost not feel.
Romeo and Juliet; 3.3.64.

Those that are betray'd do feel the treason sharply,
yet the traitor stands in worse case of woe.
Cymbeline; 3.4.83-85.

He that sleeps feels not the toothache.
5.4.170.

Feeling what small things are boisterous there,
your vile intent must needs seem horrible.
King John; 4.1.93-94.

The hardest knife ill-used doth lose his edge.
Sonnet 95

WAR

Be thou arm'd for some unhappy words.
The Taming of the Shrew; 2.1.138.

He flatters you, makes war upon your life.
Pericles, Prince of Tyre; 1.2.45.

Would we had all such wives, that the men might go to wars with the women!
Anthony and Cleopatra; 2.2.69-70.

What would you have, you curs,
that like not peace nor war?
Coriolanus; 1.1.167-168.

Honour and policy, like unsever'd friends,
i' th' war do grow together.
Coriolanus; 3.2.42-43.

War... it exceeds peace as far as day does night.
Coriolanus; 4.5.221-222.

Beware of entrance to a quarrel; but, being in,
Bear't that th' opposed may beware of thee.
Hamlet; 1.3.65-67.

Were not all unkind, nor all deserve
The common stroke of war.
Timon of Athens; 5.4.21-22

When right with right wars who shall be most right?
Troillus and Cressida; 3.2.168.

That right in peace which here we urge in war,
and then we shall repent each drop of blood
that hot rash haste so indirectly shed.
King John; 2.1.46-48

Cowards fight when they can fly no farther
Henry the VI part 3; 1.4.40.

It is war's prize to take all vantages;
and ten to one is no impeach of honour.
Henry the VI part 3; 1.4.59-60.

This battle fares like to the morning's war,
When dying clouds contend with growing light,
What time the shepherd, blowing of his nails,
Can neither call it perfect day nor night.
Now sways it this way, like a mighty sea
Forced by the tide to combat with the wind;
Now sways it that way, like the selfsame sea
Forced to retire by fury of the wind:
Sometime the flood prevails, and then the wind;
Now one the better, then another best;
Both tugging to be victors, breast to breast,
Yet neither conqueror nor conquered:
So is the equal of this fell war.
Here on this molehill will I sit me down.
To whom God will, there be the victory!
King John; 2.5.1-15.

WISDOM

To wisdom he's a fool that will not yield.
Pericles, Prince of Tyre; 2.4.54.

Love all, trust a few, do wrong to none.
All's Well that Ends Well; 1.1.57-58.

Full often we see cold wisdom waiting on superfluous folly.
All's Well that End's Well; 1.1.99-100.

Some rise by sin, and some by virtue fall.
Measure for Measure; 2.1.37

He that loves to be flattered is worthy o' the flatterer.
Timon of Athens; 1.1.228.

I swear 'tis better to be much abus'd
Than but to know't a little.
Othello; 3.3.339-340.

Thus wisdom wishes to appear most bright
When it doth tax itself.
Measure for Measure; 2.4.78-79

Love talks with better knowledge and knowledge with dearer love.
Measure for Measure: 3.2.140.

'Tis your noblest course.
Wisdom and fortune combating together,
If that the former dare but what it can,
No chance may shake it.
Anthony and Cleopatra; 3.13.78-81.

The amity that wisdom knits not, folly may easily untie.
Troillus and Cressida; 2.3.98

Wisdom cries out in the streets, and no man regards it.
Henry the IV part 1; 1.2.86.

Divorce not wisdom from your honour.
Henry the IV Part 2; 1.1.162

Wisdom be your guide.
Henry the IV part 2; 2.3.6.

YOUTH

Home keeping youths have ever homely wits.
Two Gentlemen of Verona; 1.1.2

I would there were no age between ten and three and twenty, or that youth would sleep out the rest; for there is nothing in the between but getting wenches with child, wronging the ancientry, stealing, fighting.
The Winter's Tale; 3.3.1-4.

Youth to itself rebels.
Hamlet; 1.3.44.

O foolish youth!
Thou seek'st the greatness that will overwhelm thee!
Henry the VI part 2; 4.5.97-98.

So the son of the female is the shadow of the male.
Henry the VI part 2;2.129.

BOOKS BY THIS AUTHOR

What Would Shakespeare Say? Hamlet's Words, Words, Words.

An in-depth digestion of the Bard's best lines from Hamlet. Full of fun illustrations, explanations, and examples of practical application.
A must have for any Shakespeare lover, with unique twists (Colonel Saunders of KFC makes an appearance) and even quizzes to practice your wit

You're Gonna Hurt Yourself: My Unbelievable Story Of Failure In Pro Wrestling

The author's unbelievable yet true story of attending the "ICW Hart Bros School" of professional wrestling in Cambridge, Ontario.
The book gives a detailed account of what training to be a professional wrestler is like as well as showing the emotional, mental, and physical toll professional wrestling takes. Not for the faint of heart and full of

the author's self-described demons in detail. Stories of ruined relationships, broken bones, bruised egos, and bitter disappointment. As gritty as they come and highly recommended by professional wrestlers from all levels of success.

Get A Headlock On Life: 12 Pro Wrestling Rules For Life

The only self-help book based on the unique rules of success in pro wrestling, this book is a fun survey of wrestling's greatest lessons taught by wrestling's greatest (and not so great) wrestlers, matches, and moments.

12 Pro Wrestling Rules for explains rules for success from wrestling that apply to every walk of life. Rules such as; Work your gimmick; Choose your friends carefully; Even the odds; and Work hard away from the spotlight.

The book journeys from Gorgeous George to Becky Lynch and everywhere in between via links to videos, stories from the author's personal time in business, and fun insights into what makes a professional wrestler, and a person, successful in life.

A must-have for anyone with a wrestling fan stuck on the couch or going through a run in their own life. Pure wrestling goodness in a book!

Made in the USA
Middletown, DE
01 February 2025